Down In The Valley

Contemporary Writing from the Fraser Valley

also by Trevor Carolan

POETRY
Celtic Highway
Closing the Circle

NON-FICTION
Return to Stillness: Twenty Years with a Tai Chi Master
Giving Up Poetry: With Allen Ginsberg at Hollyhock

FICTION
The Pillow Book of Dr. Jazz

ANTHOLOGIES
The Colours of Heaven: Short Stories from the Pacific Rim
The Polestar Writers Calendar Daybooks

TRANSLATIONS
The Supreme Way: Inner Teachings of the Southern Mountain Tao
(with Du Liang)
The Book of the Heart (with Bella Chen)

CHILDREN'S
Big Whiskers Saves the Cove

LIBRETTO
The Music of the Stones (with Mark Armanini)

Down in the Valley

Contemporary Writing of the Fraser Valley

Vol. 1. Writing British Columbia

Edited by Trevor Carolan

University College of the Fraser Valley

Ekstasis  Editions

Archetype West

Library and Archives Canada Cataloguing in Publication

Down in the valley / edited by Trevor Carolan.

ISBN 1-894800-59-1

1. Canadian literature (English)--British Columbia--Fraser River
Valley. I. Carolan, Trevor

PS8255.F73D69 2004   C810'.8'0971137   C2004-904407-9

Published in 2004 by:
Ekstasis Editions Canada Ltd.   Ekstasis Editions
Box 8474, Main Postal Outlet   Box 571
Victoria, B.C. V8W 3S1   Banff, Alberta ToL oCo

THE CANADA COUNCIL | LE CONSEIL DES ARTS
FOR THE ARTS | DU CANADA
SINCE 1957 | DEPUIS 1957

BRITISH
COLUMBIA
ARTS COUNCIL
Supported by the Province of British Columbia

Down in the Valley has been published with the assistance of grants from the Canada
Council for the Arts and the British Columbia Arts Board administered by the Cultural
Services Branch of British Columbia.

Preface

On the occasion of UCFV's 30th anniversary, I am pleased to acknowledge the arrival of this important first anthology of writing from the Fraser Valley. Since its inception, UCFV has regarded its educational mandate of serving the broader community as an interactive commitment, one that extends beyond teaching, and includes listening, sharing information and participating in the public discourse of the region. *Down In The Valley* celebrates this commitment by honouring the creativity, landscape, and unique human heritage which makes our shared Fraser Valley home a reflection of the Canada we're dedicated to building together.

As President of UCFV, I'm inspired to see among contributors the representation of faculty members from many of our departments, who themselves are joined by a worthy contingent of students from our university. They join with the valley's rich intercultural community of veteran and emerging poets and authors in giving this literary collection an identity which we can all recognize, and in which we can all take pride. I offer special thanks to those elders whose contribution of heritage writing bridges generations, recalling to us the dignity and labour of those whose pioneering spirit continues to thrive in this wonderful valley we call home. May you find enjoyment and merit in the pages that follow,

Dr. H.A. "Skip" Bassford
President
University College of the Fraser Valley

For the people of the Valley

They did not live to be remembered specially as noble,
…and when we praise their names,
They shake their heads in warning, chiding us to give
Our gratitude to the Invisible College of the Humble,
Who through the ages have accomplished everything
essential.

W.H. Auden

Contents

Editor's Introduction

This collection comes as the work of many hands. It took root at the 2003 Harrison Festival of the Arts' Literary Café organized by Catherine McDonald of UCFV. Just far enough from Vancouver to be genuinely regional, the Harrison Festival remains insistently cosmopolitan through its visiting international artists series and is recognized as one of the best summer festivals going. I'd long hoped for an invitation to attend. What I hadn't expected was the strength of the Fraser Valley's own writing and artistic community. There, and at other readings through the months that followed at local fundraisers, school events and the like, I kept hearing the valley's literary community find new ways to sing the old storytellers' songs, keeping them alive and vital for the times. As the poetry and prose that follows demonstrates, their work is freighted with power and humility. At its core, always there is a mosaic of emotions, vestigial ethnicities, rural imagery, and passions that arise here from a community understanding of the deep interrelatedness of things: of the mystery which comes from knowing good soil, the importance of weather patterns, about livestock, landforms; about the plants and animal life of this place.

On a clear summer day when *Kul Shan*—Mount Baker—or Mount Cheam towers over the valley and its environs, they say you can hear God breathing here. So these are writers who work from the heart. Theirs are songs that honour community and the ancient sacredness of this valley place shaped by that great salmon river, the mighty, muddy Fraser. Exquisitely local, authentically worldy, this collection of their Fraser Valley literature is a gift for which we can indeed be grateful.

I wish to especially acknowledge Jim Andersen, Bob Warick, Ron Dart, Madeleine Hardin, Barry Bompas, Virginia Cooke, Yvon Dandurand, and the administration at UCFV without whose enthusiasm and support this anthology would not have been possible. Thanks also to Richard Olafson at Ekstasis who instinctively understood the meaning of this first valley harvest. To all who contributed,

Hail to the Muse,

Trevor Carolan
University College of the Fraser Valley

Ron Dart

Sumas Energy Two Power Plant: SE2

For Patricia Ross

Most slept, warmed by work,
bread and calming circuses.
Most flitted between dawn and
dusk, the light and fight for a
better day, far from sight, soul
and soil.

She, eyes ever alert for the
right things, soul attuned to
beating things, saw and felt
shifts in the soil, a movement
that seemed not right, too right.

She lifted the conch, the Ram's
Horn high, blew long and hard,
hard, low and long. The council
and senators, initially, turned aside.
The people heard the ancient call.
They dressed for battle.

She kept the Horn close to lips,
refused to put it down. There was
a gathering, and at the gathering
much was garnered. All were told
an energy plant, if approved, would
secrete toxins into soil and soul, air
and aether, flesh and pores. Health
would falter and fail.

They had the money, the time to wait,
to wear down, water like, the rock of
resistance. The crowds grew and increased,
the gathering incensed, the script from the
Horn spoke a language that crossed tribes
and boundaries, parties and clans. This
rock would not be worn low, would stand
steady. The Horn would not go silent.

The courts, committees and councils
weighed the evidence. There was much
joy when a solid NO to SE2 was announced
by the Mayor. The Horn was not set down.
Such Horns never are.

Robert Martens

baptized

1.

it was nearly midnight when i woke up,
with an old hymn moving through my heart.
it's all memory now, but still, i feel like
i'm the lucky one. i've argued over beer
with people who have no past at all, who don't
know what's missing. as if they were born nowhere.

2.

this apartment building is commonly known as
housing for aging Mennonites. most of them
fled their real Russian homes when they were children.
i step into the lobby, and it's almost as though
i've never left. someone is belting out an old
hymn on a cranky piano. three four time,
strong, angular, relentlessly familiar.
  my hope is built on nothing less
  than Jesus' blood and righteousness.

3.

i'm making a delivery. the ladies are
arranged against the wall of the lobby,
severe posture, plain dress, gossiping in
Low German. their mother tongue. "you want
the third floor," they say in chorus, "the
elevator is to the right." i hadn't even asked.
Mennonite ladies always know exactly where to go.

4.

an old woman is waiting at her door. she
sends me an odd look, waves her hands formlessly,
she's quite deaf. "you are the martens boy,"
she says, "i know your mother." back downstairs,
as i'm leaving once again, the piano is still
proclaiming its faith. and i haven't aged a day in
all these years, i'm just the martens boy.

> *on Christ the solid rock i stand*
> *all other ground is sinking sand*
> *all other ground...*

even the power lines
(with appreciation to e.e. cummings)

the morning was grey but the music
of the heart refused to quit, sentimental
and simple, even the power lines cutting the fields
were beautiful. i felt blessed,
5   like a drowsy child. we sat together
over fried eggs and bacon, bought
coffee for another blessed one, a long ago
face half-remembered, now faltered with
Huntington's, random chance, a gift
10   from God, then heading back through
the flats, rain closing from the west,
the satisfaction of a heavy belly, and
gloom still far away and easy, women's bones
in Coquitlam, African child soldiers, the frustrated
15   rich screwing Iraq at home, i flick on
the computer, and things get personal,
hate mail from a wounded friend; i've
wounded, too, we're all mercenaries in the devil's
own corps, laying waste to whatever
20   we can't have. i don't feel very
blessed anymore, a little hatred goes a long
way. later there's talk over coffee,
aimless caffeine lifts my mood,
fake joy, chemical high, but i want
25   to sing it now, because the mood will go,
the sky will still be grey, thanks
anyway for most this amazing day,
23   thanks for the love, thanks for the hate.

[handwritten annotations: something noisy and annoying; 2 people; diner, Denny's?; after church; old friend with a disease; unlucky; "Either sarcastic irony or feeling the person is such"; life is good, but just for him.; We all have evil; selfish.; self-shaming; Unhappy; God?; 3 blessed.; 6 Religious mentions.]

Yarrow, Vedder Mountain

it seemed bigger in the morning, as though it had
grown while we slept. sharp and clear as a
blade of grass, so close you could feel it
on the skin. by afternoon, a simple
existence. it could be climbed. the Mennonite village
below went about its business. when the sun
set, it faded, hovered, a dusty red. the
street noise was hesitant, sleepy. then,
another end. below the stars, an enormous black
space where a mountain once had been. like a
bear to a child, a mother bear, watching over us,
darker than night. this is when the
hymn must be sung, the sermon unveiled.
cattle plodding home, clumsily, through memories.

one day, the streets are empty, the magic
blown away into land unknown, eastward.
our village of impossible yearnings, gone. we
have travelled a long way, you and i, through
centuries without snags or signposts. and
behind us, at night, rises the mountain.
as it has always been. a distance
so high and deep, it can only
be filled with grace.

MARION QUEDNAU

Assessment: Small Farmhouse in the Fraser Valley

Pirouette, once
and then you've said it all.
The man named Jake Somebody
came to your back door to assess
the subtleties of floors and doorways,
a delicate shifting, as yet, unrevealed,
in your 1919-vintage house
with its long-ago summer kitchen
and north-facing dreams, higher
ceilings and open hearth, still,
its wooden shorings-up
of this porch or that portico.
You weren't really at home
although you led him reluctantly
through all the rooms, and noticed
his ash-blonde eyelashes,
just like a character in your unfinished novel.
Come in, you said, meaning
the fictional world, and he seemed shy
or undecided;
you would need
to give him a motive, perhaps love.
Oh, that's been done before,
you thought to yourself as your own sturdy house
faded from sight and the stranger
drove carefully backwards
down the drive in a mild winter,
feeling already like spring.

Which One of Us, in White

We have not yet begun –
this brazen heaping of spring snow
      so bitterly cold
even the chastened warblers
and Stellar's jays, small finches at the feeder
have nothing to say –   Cards,
for example, we have not yet
played *Kings in the Corner*, or *Crazy Eights*.
      We have not given occasion
to a stirring of hot chocolate
the old-fashioned way, with clumped cocoa,
milk simmering in a saucepan.
          Or spoken of our mothers, for that matter.
The old board games – *Scrabble, Monopoly?*
Who *is* tending Park Place these days,
taking over the Burlington & Ohio Railroads,
dabbling with uneasy luck in high-spirited
scrimmage at the boundaries
      of what we have long named
"the real world"?
          Who is inventing unscrupulous
words just to see the look of astonishment
on another's face? *Carab?* (Yes, that beetle
the Egyptians laid over the hearts of corpses.)
You don't believe me?
Scarab then.
      (Or *sarcophagus.*)

      We have strayed so far
from the quiet, white kernel
folded inside
      the wider scene of buried
lawn chairs and garden hose in the mounting
snowdrifts surrounding the house –

                we could scarcely now
find enough scarves and mittens,
even imagine
         lying down and making angels
in the crystalline gardens, our foolish faces
tilted toward the steep air above,
the snow sliding (in small shocks)
up our spines in our curious
flapping, and flapping.
                     We are no longer
prepared to leave our marks, here
and here, fledgling shapes,   shuddering.
It's a shame to think there is not even
one toboggan being readied in our heads
for such white slopes.
                And last night,
          when the power went out,
which one of us
watching stopped clocks, stunned
by the prospect of a creeping chill on all the floors,
the window panes frozen by morning,
        which one of us
not yet deserted by the will
                   for this profound weather
crept to the fireplace with the as yet
untouched bag of marshmallows,
and started up a smart fire;
              which one leapt outside
as if on a glorious hunch, haunted
by some childish or ancient
oracle –
        tore at the limbs of the aching trees,
        brought in from the cold
a tribe of sharp, pointed sticks?

Whether

It was clearly a forked spring;
winter had not yet delivered,
      summer might come twice.
The she-dog had mated with her brother;
her offspring would be a twosome,
one a black-faced shivering pup,
      the other an innocence
that would never live until morning.
There was a dawn that seemed like day's end;
lightning had already struck
      the second-to-highest ridge –
those dwelling by the river's divide

saw the steep air grow white with a shattering hail
and abandoned their safer houses
with a thirsting, beneath the slant sky,
for omens –
      some even danced.
There would be softer hours, seemingly
without amaze;
      those caught in the openness
swore they saw walking fishes, and a pride
      of dark caracals, long extinct,
pacing among the handsome dead –

spoke of the awkward joy
      in *having been found,*
knew two languages in their sleep,
loved themselves,
        and still another.

Seconds

Everything in twos, the pink geraniums
on the sill, a neat matched set
of sister and brother, both absurd
and tending toward violence,
your plum-coloured socks and two winters
already without any lovers.
Surely this is begging some question.
Twice. Once should be enough,
as in being born or dying.
The story in between is perhaps a mistake
it is so mumbling and uncertain
and too often repeated.   Snap, snap;
even the crackling sounds in your head
at night when the visions begin,
mostly in recurring dreams
on parallel tracks to real living,
come at you fast like a gun's reporting
at some distance, and then,
once more, close at hand.

Al Rempel

It Was in the Way Things Moved

it was in the way things moved
and the willow leaves knew it
silver-turned in the wind, arms
stiffening as summer took the corner.
the clouds were all lit up roses
and oranges as they sped south
we can still make it, sure, sure
but remember my astronomy prof
who said there is no still point
in the whole damn universe
what cannot be shaken will remain
and the autumn leaves fall along
with what we called snow apples —
planted by *opa* in 1942—
names forgotten but not the taste
their insides whiter than sin removed.
how can it be that everything orbits
something else, yet seems so slow,
so that opa could taste the same
apple on a crisp evening and place
his palm on the same set of stars
we call the big dipper, hung by polaris
which makes the same set of rounds?
I laughed then, strung out my winters
like the beads of coloured clouds
as the moon silvered the spaces between.

JOHN CARROLL

My father's taste for ice cream sodas

My father's taste for ice cream sodas
was insatiable
root beer, birch beer.
He took me to the parlors
as soon as my mouth could value
the deep space chill of the stone.
On visits to my mother's parents
in the heart of Pennsylvania
to ease the agonizing boredom
of summer in those perspiring hills
we walked each day at one o'clock
"uptown" as the natives said
to the parlor for our oasis
in the desert of inertia.
Those distances that stretched
and reached between us
from then until this moment in
the history of our universe
contracted when
the straw touched the syrupy bottom
the reservoir of sweetness
and we both
in harmony
musicians playing our tribal horns
slurped and gurgled in satisfaction
the last remains of a fine soda
in a thick glass
licked our spoons, our lips,
wiped our mouths with tiny napkins
walked home in the heat,
a continent of glacier in our bellies,
his warm hand encompassing my own.

*insatiable root beer
or
insatiable / root beer,*

After Po Chu-i

The snow has been chased from Cheam.
Surely the dog days have come,
the wild barley gone to seed.
The lilting summer light has wilted
to a thinner thread,
the slopes always fresh
above the stalag streets,
the gaudy signs, meretricious wares,
the circus of steel on tires
as a thousand dreamers roll through –
five corners, Cottonwood,
the constrictions of Vedder Road —
but towards the mountains,
space and purest solitude!

At the Centre

Here is the danger—
that you're at the centre,
an isolate planet
encompassed by space
Just you know the secret
of orbit and spin
the lives of all creatures
are centered in you
the forests and mountains
the rocks at your feet
you are their keeper
your gravity summons
the meek and the strong
decisions come easy
you finger their fate
then inward they topple
the young and the ancient
they fall like forever
their ending is nil
but you at the centre
are untouched by losses
the centre is perfect
it may not be moved
it lives like a furnace
of nuclear starlight
it burns its own substance
consuming its soul
believing in nothing
but what is the centre
untouched by worlds
that it bends to its fate
alone and in darkness
Yes, God is great.

In a corn field, a wide puddle

In a corn field, a wide puddle.
Still, it mirrors immaculately
the alabaster mountains
and the blank sky,
so faithfully, the eye is frozen
to the copy.
Yet this world's sky is too mutely eloquent
revelatory of a depth deeper
than the roots of stubble
than the nothing in the face of its twin.
Its chalky eloquence is a dart to the eye
and on to a rather raw region of the brain
that recoils from this reflection
because it testifies its power
like a cry of emotion.
The true mountains and sky soothe
with their familiarity—
beyond is only Washington State—
not an intimation of the soul
falling like Daedalus

into the brilliance and width of the moment.

Janet Vickers

You Have a Body I Can Touch

I love birds too but I can't hold them and
our children have been taken by their wings.

Your breath is the wind I wake to. You turn
on the fan when it's hot and squeeze lemon

into cups in the morning. When I think
your hair is just right you get it cut and

get annoyed at my diagnoses of
the world, ask me why I only see the

bad, but this is a love poem and I
think you should know that when I cry it's

for your own good and mine. My rage is what
keeps me here in the shade of your love. Your

refusal to engage in my rant is
as comforting as your Yorkshire pudding

and you are reliable as barbecue
sauce. You make things, I define them. You are

the Good Guy and your words are loaves of
bread fresh out the oven when bread is what

I need more than wine. Don't thank me when I
kiss you. It has taken thirty years to

write this.

Impermanence

Thanks to impermanence, everything is possible.
Thich Nhat Hanh

The word is impermanent.
Not permanently will it permeate a thought
or resonate from the throat. And though
it never dies, it never lives long enough
to feed itself.

A word can stick out its tongue
and draw a new conclusion, eat anything
but has no digestive track, unless it becomes
a world

of appetites. Selves eating selves impermanently.
Self not staying ever anywhere. Gone
like it was never there at all. And yet
nothing can't name a thing unless it gives.

To give is to give up what it was
then.

Sunrise on Glenn Mountain

Deep blue shades
soon define branches
against a pale grey sky.

In winter I can see through
trembling aspen to the spruce
and red cedar on the hill
as waking houses yawn

kettles in their kitchens boil
people in down comforters stretch toward
the alarm.

The Unborn Chill

On a cold morning make the bed naked
throw back the covers of your night
your folding for warmth, creature bliss
unconscious flight to blue Arcadia.

Brush flakes of skin from wrinkled sheets
you are awake now to window frost
the sky full of snow falling casually
onto pruned rose bushes and tender

exclamations of grass silenced by yesterday's
wind. See your nipples shrink and flesh
goose itself to Winter. The call is this:
some part of your life wants more than

porridge, the larding of your belly.
Some light in your grandmother's eyes
shows you how your body has become
the shape of your desires.

KRISTINE ARCHIE

'Til I Head Home

This valley isn't my first home, nor is it my last
My real home is Tsq'escen, in Secwepemcul'ecw
That's where summer days were like blankets
And from cold winter nights, grew our backbone.
We were Fierce.

Tsq'escen, Broken Rock – Once we were broken people
Now thriving, pulsating like the earths p'usmen
The heart grows strong in us st'smemelt and impts
Full of pride, stepping forth from our core.
We are Strong.

My time in Fraser's Valley has been short and gray
Full of misty rain, like my endless learning — foggy
Yet through the fog and city structures— those Mountains
They've etched themselves into my core.
They are Eternal.

My core, my sanctuary from that city-pavement-hell
Has tigerlily-sage-wildness for my pillow
The golden-sundried-hay is my bed
With the ancestor-shining-stars, my blanket
This is Real.

The Valley has become an embrace, the walls of my core
I am welcomed into the strength of their p'usmen
The rhythmic beat tells me I'm home
Right now—here—until I head back to Tsq'escen
We are One.

> *Secwepemcul'ecw* - Land of Secwepemc
> *p'usmen* – heart
> *st'smemelt* - children
> *impts* - grandchildren

ROSE MORRISON

Hiking Mount Cheam in August

Foot trudges after foot.
Mouth imbibes valerian-incensed air.
Mind submits to insects' thrumming hymn.
Body grudging, starts its pilgrimage.

Halfway up
face seared by sun.
A pew of rock gives respite.
Right here, the slab of Lady Mountain,
to south, the peak-rimmed sky.
Spoon Lake below, transmutes to lapis lazuli.
Hands, searching ground, come back stained with blueberries.

Past penstemon, past paintbrush,
mimulus and Indian pipe.
Glacier lilies portend
mold-pink snow
that teases tongue and quenches breasts with cold.

A thousand things that were left undone
and a thousand done in wrong
are plodded out in penitent toil.
And tears of sweat
find rest
in merciful soil
as the pilgrim's health is won.

then

Holy wind
sweeps through
the nave of Mount Cheam.
The pilgrim stops.
The backpack drops.
Spirit rushes in.

Revisiting Hong Kong with my father

Remember Lan Tao, Po Lin and Cheung Chau?
Look at the mainland and how it has changed.
On the boat, your voice came to me on the wind.

I walked in Kowloon, along paths that are past
and your hand was on my shoulder.
Tall apartments have grown from the ground of our house.
See where the garden's strong walls used to stand?
You laughed then, recalling flowers and the dog that you loved.

Your sound was soft on the shores of Hebe Haven.
Watch how the water laps over my ashes -
once more and once more and again.

How can you still be here when
many years ago, you met the woman on the bridge
and drank the soup of all-forgetting?

RICK MAWSON

My Tomato

I don't trust my tomato.
She displays
all the blushing imperfections
of an airbrushed centerfold, yet
her firm, rotund flesh
conceals a perverse mystery,
conceived in a test tube.

She has been coerced
into unnatural acts
in a nursery,
by scientists
driven mad by the bottom line.
Her crimson womb
penetrated
by a surreptitious syringe.

Once our oral love play was
delicious.
Now when I probe her
secret centre,
I am
unsatisfied.

My tomato has a number.
It is 4763.
She is barren.
Insects avoid her.

Could I learn to love her again?
Some slight sign of decay,
a brief blemish,
a lack of symmetry,
hinting at imperfect fecundity = *Reproduction.*
might rekindle my desire.

But for now
I fear a seedless future,
and crave
the minstrel
taste.

Jab at organic vs. non-organic foods?

CRISPIN ELSTED

Bosnia

Ubi solitudinem faciunt, pacem appellant.
They make a desolation, and they call it peace
Tacitus, AGRICOLA

They make a desolation and they call it peace,
blast hollows where hills spun in light, call peace
absence of action, where things occur
apparently native, like a violet spur
that bruises purple springing from a split
wall in a vacant house. Fright here
slipped violent in the air
like a hawk's shadow
slopped in pools and skewed
the apprehension of rocks, of a house
where a man who was a father stood
and thought as his body came apart
a witness said, like water
from a fall, farther than yesterday. Lichen
on dry stone blooms. It all,
every thing, falls in on its own
self same loss. Say this
what it is, not compare it idly
to some lovely thing.
Look a child in pieces is not peace
because it does not cry. A place
where nothing grows gives no trouble
it can give nothing.

If there is music in rubble
loosening, falling together, struck
hope, music means that words
can find no way to say:
Stop. Name this. Call it
what we cannot bring ourselves to kill.
You have named this desolation peace.
Name it desecration, and be still.

Infelix simulacrum

quaerenti et tectis urbis sine fine furenti
infelix simulacrum atque ipsius umbra Creusae
visa mihi ante oculos …

ter conatus ibi collo dare bracchia circum;
ter frustra comprensa manus effugit imago,
par levibus ventis volucrique simillima somno.

As I rushed, searching endlessly, frantically, from house to house,
there rose in my sight the sad shadow and ghost of Creüsa herself

three times I tried to throw my arms around her neck, three times
her form, like a light wind, a winged dream, sighed from my clasp.

Virgil, AENEID, II

Remember, as I will, how my hand
lay on your breast like light breaking over a sill
to a house long loved and deserted.
Had it been a song, it would have been sung
around leaves, near water, between shadows
as the whisper of a hand stroking skin near dawn.

Remember sometimes in tallow heat
a cool slip of wind, a kiss like a bird
lingering, choosing a branch particular
and thinned in the geometry of dawn.
Day broke obtuse, acute, like a heart
if you recall, on the sill of the room

where we lay enrobed in one another.
Well, we may remember or forget.
It may not be given to choose. Perhaps
in the long damp season where we lose
ourselves, puzzling through mornings
in which no words can reach the shelf

where between the leaves of a half-read book
the meanings lie, you may turn in bleached light
toward me, hoping for my hand
on your breast, thinking me asleep,
dimly seen against a fence
far down the field of your thinking

so that you must stroke your hair back from your eyes
to see me. As you hold my head
against your shoulder, your thoughts in mine,
I know your hands break the surface
of reflection. The threads of first light
flutter out from the pane onto the sheet

of the day. Our bodies move, shift, sweeping
their curves into habitual corners, shifting
the silken grit of delayed, discarded thoughts
in a dim sweet harp of light, a fumbling slim
thumb of light that strums the trees. (*There was
no rest, no, nor grace before music, nor light*

*that sacramental day, when she was carried
up some wretched beach never so graced before,
dull and filled with water. The idle hands
of the foreshore reached from their frayed cuffs
to poke and prod her. She was, my love,
hymns in long metre, Babylon's streams,*

light declining.) And where she is
no longer, you are. There
in desperation in the dawn at a lake, where
there should be no desperation, you are
left to heal me. I can offer
a random welcome, evident as swans and soft

as ashes on the air, for I have come to love you
through the streets of the years. Your wrists
are links to my touch, your eyes
flower and swell as I search them out, your temples
set serenity to speech, your neck is a round music.
I know no other loveliness. Your breasts are warm.

I would wish to bring you
to a folly of joy roosted in the thorns of a morning.
But mercy is culpable kindness. May your gift to me
be yourself, a violet in moss, damp
and nestled in the cup of your loins, touched
by your retiring, your silence, a secret benefice.

I am moved by your honour,
the discipline of your affections,
but charity and the need for mercy are
welcome and abiding. Well, enough.
Now from the petals comes the purple
of morning scents. The nail of crows

scratches the sheen of dawn
toward some havoc, tuning polity
from insolence with their plangent courtesies.
You endear yourself to your own end, like a candle
brightest when my eyes are anywhere but on you,
loveliest in my sight. Over our bodies' fine mischiefs, night

peels its sticky shade from rocks and trees.
We have shifted into a pain not properly ours.
But as branches of blossom turn aside lean winds
we may, in time, set by. You will divine
my meaning. We shall lie straight and limp
in the strong earth of recollection.

Such admonitions are the work of charity.

Woman, & Woman with Music

1.

I have squandered you with my eyes until you are spent.
Your thoughts' quick waters tumble over their beds
like starlings in flocks falling into trees at dusk.

Quick fingers you have, that shake out your hair
into the paddock of ease. Your mouth
turns its smiling loose to lope and attend
and your eyes are the colour of bells. Teach me,

show me the way of giving and receiving, how you open
all of yourself to the grazings of love, for all that I know.
Teach me the tense eternity in which you cast
the verbs of everything you say, for I have no words
worth even your aspen laughter turning the light to account.

To my eye you are lovelier than sight, as birdsong
hangs laburnum on the air, as trees heaved by the wind
make walkers dance. I spend your beauty to discover it.
Like a cripple I walk with the sight of trees heaving.
A grosbeak's song hangs golden in the air.

2.

All women hearing your music drop their eyes
as if the song were a sudden wonder
bringing you to yourself, a music whose lines
gleam silver in a garden, a web holding
a fence and a flower unalterably together, too delicate
to sing after the music is gone.

You hear how the hissing fall of lupins mown away
untunes the moment, and see they are not spring's flowers
for all they bear its colours – no more may gentleness
tear tawed brutality.

Now night comes down in the high tune of the clock.
Now the owls slide down the moon's light arms like cloth
and night stands quiet as stars undo her dress.

You know that tears are not expected, are come
to correct what seemed to be joy, or was, you know
that we must use the rain to part us from them, that a grief

wraps itself in parcels of light that tumble into the dark.
Secretly I leave words in your hands, so that when you
see your hands you read them, whether or not I am there

as if I had kissed their palms.
                                        Happiness is to be learned
or got by habit, and whiteness and straightness are the same for you
as for the finches searing the shadow of that pine.

Of the flight of any bird we may say that it shows
partiality, of the walk of any dancer that it steps into
the order of signs, of the heart's inclining
that it is a simple of prudence. The path is straight.
The path is white and long and many times described.

Of gentleness & nightfall, and of love
we take our accustomed exercise.

CAMERON LITTLE

Weekend Pursuit

It's bitter cold.
Our breath hangs in the wind.
The kick-off is high and deep.
Game on.

Jon is playing today.
Doctors and X-rays could not hold him back.
"What of tomorrow?" we ask.
"Tomorrow can wait—the game is now."
Machismo in buckets.

Soon bodies feel not the weather.
Our pursuit keeps us warm.
Relentless is the chase.
The ball is doomed.

A last minute touchdown.
Victory!—A yelp of pain.
Jon is injured again.
He'll play next week.
Just as we all would in his place.

The days move slowly.
Cold, wind and frost loom in the distance.
It will not stop us.
The ball shakes in fear.

Ranbir Banwait

Alienated

Fierce pride, fearlessness, and poverty;
Those things that kept them together
In turn tore them apart.

Pride, respect, and honour
Upheld the symbols of valour
For which they fought in the sandy lands
Of the ancient civilization.

Fearlessness: it was the urge to win the symbol of
Honour that drove the fights of blood,
Fought for pride's sake
Against the reality of humanity.

Poverty: it was that uniting force against the
Conditions of life, that united those linked
In blood, against those with the courage
To challenge them.

Known in the land as those brothers and sisters
Who stand, their unity was their strength.
Death of a brother weakened that fist,
And life captured the cracks in love
That already existed.

Their move to this land once again
Strengthened the bond of purpose—
Struggles, poverty, and fights of honour.

But wealth, success, and independence, finally
Dissolved the fist of brothers and sisters:
Poverty to greed
Love to hate
The instinct to protect
Gave way to internal struggle.
Splintering bonds and fragmenting relations
Captured in the remnants of broken glass.
Destroyed faith, and bitter memories.

Lived in, lived by, and to die with
Poverty, fearlessness, and fierce pride.
Those things that kept them together
In turn tore them apart.

Values of the East

Built on the foundation of hopes
Traditions and nurtured dreams
Is a life lived, and then lost
With the passage of time.

Values, Culture, and its beliefs
Give life to another generation
Raised with laughter and pride:
A doctrine of honour and love.

Go venture into the world
And make us proud
You our children whom we raised
With the toil of our hands.

And return to us, remember
The values of the East.
Be with us,
To lay our ashes on the sea.

…And then they return
The epitome of success, wealth,
And Education:
Home they have reached.

Products of indifference,
In pursuit of life and leisure
Liberty and loose ties
Forgotten cultural beliefs,

They leave behind a temple of ruins
Fleeting ghosts, laughing echoes
Loneliness for companionship
And seeking eyes lost
In yesterday's dream.

NOLA ACCILI *Pretty*

The Vegetarians

how about Grandpa's rabbits
oozing on the white Beetle hood
or an osculating moose

us just eight, laughing
thinking the silly lamb (we named him Oogles
on the car ride home)
is being tickled in the backyard

voices full of ontology shout for
rags, cigarettes, jugs of wine

we're too busy stringing tinsel
on the antlers in the driveway
sticking carrots in the puckered gray
rabbit mouths

craving at least one of them awake

To say I get it

the smell of varnish coming from a neighbour's driveway
"like-new" cabinets mingled with cigarette smoke
or a slap in the face ?   *Bad smells maybe?*

and what you didn't say
when all I craved was a piece of syntax   *I don't know what*
sliver of velvet on an oozing sore   *Image for*   *this means?*
soft   *sharp pain*
and the sound of wind chimes
from that balcony next door
where a cat lies dozing in a hammock

instead it was the musty confessional   *go to the church*
old men half-dazed listening while   *to talk it out.*
unravelling their beads
                    ~~blurry~~ *blurry gendered*
or androgynous therapists   *a real by the book, boring man*
drunk with method
looking up and down my skirt *analyzing*

                    Purpose of religion
what's the point of our ornate cathedrals
Tuscan landscapes flowing with geraniums
that actually smell like something

all in a black hole now   *Talking about*
being batted across constellations   *some guy.*
we never saw anyway

*All of these wonderful images and REAL LIFE
moments and it is all shut down at the end...
A very profound poem   Zoom out.
Bring it down to an astronomical level*

READ BETTER 51 *Didn't read this
one right. Try again*

KULDIP GILL

Blueberry Fields - Matsqui

Soon, the blueberry field's furrows
now bark-mulched ankle deep, will shine
with a dusting of snow, the tracks of the farmers
Nikes, mixed with bird feet imprinted one
over the other. In India, I've seen cloth block-printed
by hand, patterned similar to this field. Row
on row, the symmetry slightly askew as humans
are wont to do. At the ends of the rows,
the aqua-coloured nets are rolled, now
their valiant attempt to keep starlings out,
finished for another 'blues' ripening season.
The farmer's wife shivered as she loosened them
from the nets, broken-wings all a-flap. Recalls,
she whispered over and over: ahimsa, ahimsa.

Mrs. Spilsbury at the Plough - Whonnock, 1911

Cedar trees, two rows
of twenty-three upright four-by-sixes frame
the Spilsbury house in black outline against the sky.
Four props assist the house until the house is built.
Uncut logs lay strewn across the yard and down the hill.
Mrs. Spilsbury holds a set of reins and he, the handles
of the plough. The two horses pull, their feet planted,
necks arched, as they roll over another furrow of rocks,
earth and mangled root bundles. Sikh men watch, stopped
in their tracks by Mrs. Spilsbury in white blouse, straw hat
and long skirt, as she stalks along the furrow shouting
Gee Hah!, as she slaps the reins on the horses' flanks.

The four turbaned men stand relaxed,
their arms hang loose from their shoulders, perhaps
astounded by her resolve. They have propped up *Spilsbury
House.* The studs stand straight up on either side of the floor,
leveled with one side flush on the ground, the other raised
and supported by a foundation of upright logs. It is nineteen
hundred and eleven. Four Sikhs in coveralls stand watch
at Mrs. Spilsbury and her team at the plough.

Grandpa Charlie Saunders

Peevee, pike pole, boom chain
Grandpa Charlie Saunders didn't
swim, his boots laced up his legs
so tight, he dared the Old Fraser
River to leak in. All his life he walked
the logs and the few times he fell
into the Fraser he propelled himself
back up again like "a shot out of hell"
onto the boom as if the devil himself
spit him out of the river-bottom's
tides and eddies.

In spite of those potential anchors
in his hands draggin'
him down, and the boom chain
around his neck, he refused to let go,
he clutched them as if they could
float. His own pike pole,
peevee, and chain, his right arm.
Swim, or not-swim-be-damned,
every time he fell in, he leapt
out of the water right on to
the boom again. Allyoop.Charlie,
You're goddamn right!

The Burnt House Stands, a Ghost

The wind ruffled the creek water
a pointillist painting of the lights
and shadows of the cottonwood and
the wild river willows. The families
of Canada geese floated towards
the edge where the creek spilled
over the banks, and flooded the meadow
over the knees of the wild rose
bushes and blackberry thickets.

There the burnt house stands, a ghost
among the rampant grasses, and even so
the lily perennially blossoms, oblivious
in its lonely vigil. The tenants long gone,
sorrowing their loss of home and belonging,
left the apple, pear and plum to their skirts
of daffodils, astilbe and long-limbed daisies,
dandelion, dill, and wild clover. And the clothes
drying stand lies tilted over, with broken and loose
plastic strings, the bleached bones of wooden clothes
pegs, dangling skeletal shreds of linen skin
as it blows leathery in the wind.

A lone boy cycles along the dike with his fish
tackle bag slung over his back, a packet of matches
in his hand, surprised to see me and the dog,
stops to ask if he can get to the river's edge by taking this
road along the creek. A private road. A burnt house.

Pitt Lake Ghazals for the Drowning

Sometime in the late 1950s, some of Mission's finest young married and single men who logged in the area, were drowned as they took their small boat up to the logging camp. I knew some of them and their families.

I.

> *How admirable!*
> *to see lightning and not think*
> *life is fleeting.*
> Basho

Deadheads, rooted without roots in putrid brown water. They don't wave as grasses. They are staunch. One end up and one down.

They loom in dark water waiting. Deadheads don't wave, they lie in wait dark foggy white or pinky fog mornings. Teething,

drowned five loggers! Who were they? Who were they? Loggers going back to camp from two nights on the town.

A townspeople—scurry. Oh! God—it was Hank. And Who? And Who? And Who? And, who else went down? Five men, townsmen with him.

Their boat! Who steered the boat, chainsaws, gear? In black early-morning
fog haze on Pitt Lake. Deadheads. Deadheads that wait and wait without a wave.

II.

The cold mountain water. Ice. The boat, its crack and thud into that raised 'head', feet planted in mud, unrelenting, never floating, aeons.

Five men flew for moments, landed wet. Heavy feathers, sink and sink. Prized chainsaws, metal toed logging boots, the week's food, and a deck of cards.

A logger afraid of woods. He fled them once. The dark arms that reached out to him. But he went back in. O'Hara's horseman rode to that meeting place.

Drive by Pitt Lake, it darkens and darkens with deadheads of thought rising, rising here and here and there! See those Mission men, the town remembers again.

Now. Forty years or two score and the half of ten. The kisses on that chimera of a morning as she turned, not wanting to wake, still. Still yearning as he went.

Michael Aird

Boat in a Grass Field

Like the things that happen to us,
like water, being that
arid summer months, and some
moments stalling their particular
time and place.

Anger almost invites vegetation,
growing steadily still
only an accident
imposing otherwise
perceived so.

It's really the 12 phenomenal
feet, the paint
flaked where there was something S. S. once,
and then absence itself,
enlarging into

nothing but limits,
into the catch we've walked through
previous to just
arriving at today's field
(perceptions otherwise).

Not what this boat wants, what
it would say about ownership, or
salvation matters—the lake
will always be
inconstant, an ally perhaps.

But what is said, and written
down somewhere, will
contradict finally ideas
of a shortcoming, thought
about as second nature.

A third exists if
even continuing doesn't—
doubtless
to get away was the big one's
only choice.

J. M. BRIDGEMAN

Milk and Honey

In her black and white world
Honey eats, Honey chews; she
rests, she produces, she
reproduces
more contented cows.
From valley floor
she lifts
her Bride eyes
to the green
pacific hills.

Bridal Falls

Through arching green boughs draped with silver moss we ascend to the granite rockface washed with whitewater cascading in tiers from invisible Source to the tumbled boulders below. The rustle of this billowing train whispers in the echoing nave.

We have hiked this trail before. Skirting the Pixie Cups and Fairy Slippers. Tending the Shooting Stars. With child ears I still hear her telling me the understory—Five Fingers, Maidenhair, Bracken and Swordferns. With her eyes I first did see bruised white blossoms 'neath the canopy dappled with growth and decay.

In this box of polished cedar I carry the woman who carried me. Defying the signs, I leave the path, break a pungent trail through fallen timber. Beneath the nurse log suckling twins, I sprinkle her into beckoning Ghostfingers, onto pallid Angel Wings. With the mist rising from Bride's veil, she vanishes into the tapestry of the grove.

I step through the falls into a shaft of light and return alone to the plain.

My mother is not. She is moss. She is cedar. She is jade. I am no one's daughter. I am a space in the lace of Bride's crown; I am shadow dancing in the shimmer of brocade. I am willow pining, water winding home below the falls. I am Dogwood centred from all the trees—in a rush of confusion as the nails enter. Say you have chosen, not forsaken me. Tell me this pain is ecstasy.

The Source
(aka Mt. Cheam)

She is

THEETH-uhl-kay

the Peak

from whom the Waters Spring

with

I-oh-wat   and   Say-oo-WAT

her Daughters

above

Chee-AH:M   Wild Strawberry Fields

and

STAW-loh, the River

Mother Mountain

Mother Mountain

Mother Mountain

Rock

Me

ALVIN G. ENS

Mole Hills

Except in mating season,
the mole is a loner,
aggressively territorial,
and eschews even its own kind.
This fact of isolation alone
should ensure its extinction
in one generation.

With no mating moose call,
or coyote's serenade,
no nocturnal forays
over vast territory,
its tunnel to love
is slow and silent.
This fact alone should
ensure its extinction
in one generation.

One lone human, I,
with far superior intelligence,
mobility and resources,
aggressively hunt the mole
under my lawn.
This fact alone
should ensure its extinction
in one generation.

It forages a mere four inches
below me with its pointy snout,
and thumbs it at me
with little hills of haughtiness.
What knowledge or instinct,
what sonar capacity,
what survival skills?
I set another trap.
This fact alone
is God's sense of humour
to keep me humble.

PEGGY SUE NEUFELD

Dawn's Day for the Setting Son

For Dawn Crey, and for her 49 missing sisters
In memory

Dawn came in the early morn
Sun splintering,
Edging over the Fraser water
Spontaneous spits of liquid purging itself
Upon the rocks;
Crey's fish flapping against the side of the boat
Brutally bashing its tail into the wood,
Cleaving
Spewing, eclipsed beyond repair
Eagle's prey upon the back of Crey.
Pig's eyes
Tantalize evil in their response to tears
The Dawn watches with statue hands
Reaching out …pressing past the pig's stare,
Beyond to the goodness that once was in her grasp.
Her palms feel the nails that bled her Savior's flesh;
She presses up beyond the pain
Pure light injects her soul
Her elders stand with soft strength.
She's anticipated this grand day—
Oh, the trip was so awful to
Endure upon the black wings of pigs …to here.
Love is everywhere inside her head.
Great Creator, "Let me enter this time."
She turns to look at the hellish site,
Down, down, so…below …her now;
No measure for the insanity,
No cup for their device.

She has risen past the last birth canal;
Tricks, torture and temptation
Securely cast aside.
Beauty clothes each move she makes,
Peace magnified into her soul.
True labor of love
The past …to present …passages.

Smiles greet her everywhere.
She falls again and giggles,
Tiny little toes become the best play things.
Upon the floor she rolls and wiggles;
Her ebony pony tail
Sways from side to side.
She just wants to nibble some salmon
Chew berries, raspberries
Bannock or pie.
Dawn curls upon my lap;
My baby you will always be…
Just rest awhile my sleepy head.
Tomorrow my little Dawn
you shall rise to meet the Son.

HILDA HARDER

Remembering When

For my brother Harry's 75th Birthday

He was always ready to help.
He liked to work
And didn't needed to be asked.
If he saw something to be done,
He did it!
He was mom's pride and joy (but she loved me too)
And me...well, I had Dad (but he loved him also)
It seems to be that way
Sometimes
When there's only two.
Harry and cousin Bill, always together
And me trailing behind,
(when they couldn't hide from me)
The kid sister,
A pest!
They climbed the highest peak
On the barn
To look at the nest
Of baby pigeons.
There I couldn't follow.
Sleeping on the front veranda in summer;
Honeysuckle vines sweet smell.
Grape arbours screen.
We felt safe, important to our parents;
And so we were.
We'd climb up on the two by fours
Nailed on my closet wall;
Walked gingerly across the rafters
To the chimney

Where the bats nested.
The bats would swoop and dive
In the evening dusk.
Harry and Bill tried to hit them
With bean poles,
But never hit a one.
The train brought men in the thirties.
Hungry men, never turned away
But given a meal and a bed of straw:
"no smoking in the barn"
was the only rule.
The old peddler, pushing his wheelbarrow display
Of needles and threads and such
Always ended his day with us,
Knowing there was a good meal
And a sleep in the barn.
After berry picking season, holidays at Birch Bay,
Boiling fresh caught crab;
Or a rented room for a week
Near Stanley Park,
Woodwards, and the White Spot.
We didn't have a car, and so we walked,
Picnicking at the cool waterfall
At the base of the mountain
Swimming at Pages Lake,
Picking blackberries and wild hazelnuts.
Always time for friends and neighbours.
Cousins loved to come!
Vaudeville family down on their luck
Entertained us with song and dance;
All met with happy acceptance.
I suppose that we were poor,
But now looking back
Through the years,
In the things that really mattered
We were rich indeed!

DOUG ISAAC

Missing in Inaction

Before it's over
discredits roll
and lights are up
from seasoned flesh
I want to purge
salt stains of melodrama
re-do the music track
put in heavy metal
weepy country, rap
peel calluses from
writhing tendril tips
of moldy soul
bleed a little, maybe
a lot in hemophiliac
emotion, feel
potholes, bumps
and on Old Yale Road
where the macadam
ends, and means
we're off the beaten
track, there, I would
finger ochre photochemical
Lower Fraser August sky, brew
stew in old juice cans
see sounds of time
cut my punctured palms
on blades of grass
write my own Pro-Choice
bristleboard signs, prove
perspective was a lie
that all telephone

poles were the same
size, no matter how
far away. I'd make my own
chokecherry wine, cut my own logs
of random thought
useless information.
Thus unhindered, dis-
informed, perhaps, then
I'd find the *Missing*
In Inaction, buried
in a Matsqui flood plain bog
up to the neck.

The Forger

You are rubbed out
of the picture, you claim
in hindsight was a forgery.
Each ermine-brush stroke of love
shade of understanding
line of interdependence
faked, you insinuate, done
by an accomplished master
of the form. (All forms
are part of the same vanity –
an attempt to render
underlying reality, or, grander yet
essential truth.) A con was on
both sides, neither would admit
though the gilt framing
was elaborate, hard-edged
along the inside
perimeter.

My take on melodrama
differs from yours – bathos
vs pathos, sunset against moonrise.
Our celluloid moved too fast
sprocket holes were shredded
frames burned through.
In fast forward you could not
pixillate, choosing to revert
to your *Mennisten* chains
forged along South Fraser
Way: the books must balance
however unbalanced minds
and hearts might be.

My forgery – if I accept
your myopic view – exuded more
authenticity than the Tiffany'd
window of our Bakerview
Mennonite Church,
than your pillory
by the bottom-line.
Double-entry (quick-in
like us both:
quick-out, like you)
is your mucilage.
You didn't get it –
but it was I who came
unglued.

The (Frozen) Tyger *(With effusive apologies to William Blake)*

Globe & Mail Headlines: *"Frozen zoo would confine rare tiger
species to cells... Siberian Tigers face frosty future."*

Tyger! Tyger! your future's a frozen dab
stored deep in freezers of the basement lab.
What hubris-ridden man or firm
Could freeze thy hyperactive sperm?

In what jungle or Siberian plain
Burnt your lust to sire again?
In what petrie dish did they aspire,
After rectal probing to steal thy fire?
The (Frozen) Tyger
In the cause of cryogenic preservation,
is a frozen zoo your best salvation?
Yet, when thy courageous heart begins to fade,
with embryonic transplants immortality is made.

Why the cages? Why the chain?
In what freezer lies thy brain?
What rationale? Why not let you free?
Instead of quick-freezing your progeny?

When genetic engineers let go facades,
they say, "Let's flog this sperm, thru internet ads."
Do they rejoice in reproductive physiology,
concocting time-bombs, while preserving thee?

Tyger! Tyger! your future is a frozen dab
stored deep in freezers of the basement lab.
What immoral hand or eye
Dare freeze thy fearful symmetry?

from: Sailing to Exurbia

Cool Pillow

you sleep, embracing
my cool
      pillow,
indulging
      my nights
insomniac scribbling

      or terror
      unknown to you
        despair
        unwanted
      fantasies of self
      destruction or plastic
      surgery
        augmented
      with dreams of success
      that eludes me
      the way a firm grip
      on 3 a.m. fabulations
        of moonlight
      touches reminiscent
      of simple joy
        slip
      into the folds
      of my atrophying soul
      dissolve in tears, repeated
      butts with calloused forehead
      against white seamless drywall

I try to gore, hook
incisively, strike with verve
insight, the right keys
        that I might
at last exit (I, too, can trace
 a woven spider's thread)

harden in our perfect fit
your body heat, my cool
pillow, flawed nights
repaired with sunrise
our laughter – together
coming

ELSIE K. NEUFELD

Moment 3

You can feel it inside when you wake. A faint shift
in each cell like a runnel of air your skin knows
is there but can't name. Bones unsettled, it's that deep
in your marrow. Dawn later each morning, birds quiet
evenings sooner and long. What's worse, early or late?

Last night you closed all the windows. Watched the sun
disappear from inside. The far purpled mountains
and clotted pink skyline merged after dark. Moths
ticking the glass white wings threshing illumined panes
resembled a frayed marmalade label. Everything's drawn
to what's absent. The light all night left on.

These days you look at gardens less often. The dirt
under dropped blossoms baked hard. A lament heard
in each colorless spot. You tell yourself nothing
is barren though it seems otherwise. What's gone
will appear again elsewhere. Those raised blue veins
on hands that resemble your mother's. Thin stripes
of gill-silver tracks on your buttocks and belly. Benign
birthmarks. The skin is a calendar-clock.

This is the time you wished for, wanted
never to come. The world in Fall as a spent flame
ignited again and again till it's gone. The switch
always too sudden! You know this for certain when you start
talking to mirrors. A stranger inside remembering you
back

to those black & white photos, and your son's
question about colour on earth; when did it start?
Now, when you turn to the window you see less
singular hues. The shift within named as you imagine
slender white roots curled underground into one.
A dead fly on the hem of the curtain.

Silent Retreat

You know you've come a long distance when the rocks in your soul have turned into feathers. A wind nudging them out of your grasp to scatter them God knows where. Maybe on water, the silt brown river, a ditch or this bog where you're walking. Ducks nattering paths through bullrushes in shallows. A tabby asleep on the step of a moored houseboat. Yellow door locked. A far mill sawing day after night.

You return to the house laughing like the small girl next door. A blue-robed Mary of stone enshrined in fenced yard. Head bowed under arbor, bare feet bangled with a red snake and these words: Immaculate One. The new Eve. Arms wide, her hands cupped over offerings below: an old stump, brass chalice, a polished gray boulder. Lamb's Ear grazing her hem, a white moth at her elbow. Applause or escape? Are you happy, Mother of God, Holiest Mother of all?

Cloud shadows travelling rooftop and garden. Kelly the dog finally quiet. This is no Eden! A bonneted frog tipping faux water on silk flowers guarded by bright plastic bees, a clay Raggedy Andy & Ann and gnomes. The sad one under a pole & smiling one stood in a corner. Glazed eyes looking up. Lawn sprinkler hissing as if water is air and what's dead worth reviving.

Birds pecking the loose ground near the still feet of Mary. She's blind sees it all. The nun rolling her eyes as she chats about weeds, her desire for help and wish to shed weight. She can't erase either! Her poodle beside her humping the cat toy she gave him a loud squeal all day long of jets descending above The Grey Sisters' Silent Retreat House.

The Saw's Song

They like to go in at the end
of winter when the ground's still
damp and tree roots rained in
the thick brush a shroud for fumes
of diesel and chains you can hear them
from far think first it's nothing
but dirt-bikes even imagine those
wide rubber tires mud sprayed on a maze
of slim trails the old pillar trees
an emerald breeze and ferns' wave
in the pass like raised hands and suddenly
you know in the way one knows
that stutter and brazen blade's whine
then CRACK! and the felled one's fall
the dog's frantic chase after the far
ricocheted thwack; it's a terrible show!

saw on and on its serial ah ah ah turned
urgent long snarl then staccato crescendo
legato a rise and silence
did the cutter give thanks before
moving on? Earth wanting arms
as another one limb over limb tumbles
and snaps
splinters all over ants scattered
long legged beetles crushed or torn
from their covers creek's roar
and birds' delicate chirr, woodpecker's
knock and stellar's reproach lost
in the blue cough of a log hearse
coming up to get more
the saw's song again ahhhhh ahhhhhh

SHELLEY HAGGARD

Bamboo Speak

The rich, brown-black
coloured bamboo wind chime
I made for the garden,
sounds nothing like
the stand of bamboo
it came from.
Its colours, enhanced
with wax, gleam,
its wooden resonance is deep,
while the re-cycled
copper topper
has a burnished glow.
So unlike the living stalks
curving gently
under weight of bright
green fronds, fifteen
feet tall, or more.
Filtering the wind through leaves:
a small enough sound;
until it suddenly brooms
all other noises out of existence.
How I love the bamboo speak,
in either of its tongues.
How graceful and blessed
I feel to be in its presence,
like by doing so I
replicate its qualities.
How kind of the universe
to allow me this tranquil
piece of paradise,
that I can produce my own
pieces of paradise,
for those gardens not blessed
with either of these languages.

Vicki Grieve

Blackberry Duet

I. Blackberry Pie

I am making blackberry pie
the first in years
and have forgotten
how much flour and how much sugar
will thicken the juice and sweeten the sting

So I summon my mother in her blackberry get-up
    (how often she was in costume)
the kerchief covering her hair-do
and a smart but juice-stained London Fog
and my good old saddle-loafers from the 60s
en-tone with the jacket

    All the puttings-on and takings-off

Sparkling rings before she rolled out pastry
an apron to stir the gravy
earrings and nail-lacquer before going out
the not-quite-there face of early morning

I see her from a child's height
eye-level with the old Singer
as the clever fingers guide the fabric
through the presser-foot
the noise of the machine rising to a glorious crescendo
as she races to the end of the seam

The deft cutting with the scissors, sharp
as her fierce hunger for our happiness,
and love
as predictable as perfect pie

So I can hear her voice saying
one cup of sugar and two tablespoons of flour
and remember

      her measures are with me still.

   II.   The Effect of Blackberries

              Late summer,
and late middle age when our father veered off
the path of righteousness,
the highway between Harrison and Chilliwack,
and ended up, motor still running,
amongst the stalks of golden corn in a farmer's field.

              Never a wasteful man,
he gathered up the fallen cobs, put the Ford Galaxy
in reverse, backed out through his blazed trail,
found the highway and drove home.

              Well.
We were waiting, his dinner in the oven.
Golf tournament he explained, poker
and some drinks afterwards with the boys.
I brought corn, he said, but I guess you've eaten.

                    Maybe
I'll just take the dog
for a per – am – bu – la – tion.

                    Safe enough,
we thought, forgetting about the foraging—
the over-ripe peas and swollen brussel sprouts
that the combines left behind, and dandelions gathered
for syrupy wine, suspicious mushrooms we all declined
but that he would fry and eat while we watched for signs
of a slow, painful death. Delicious, he said.

                    That night
we underestimated the effect of blackberries,
beckoning like sirens from the uneven slope
along the lee-side of the dyke where he walked,
four sheets to the wind, weaving in the dusk.

                    He came back
with his good shirt ripped and stained, blood
from the gouges on his face and arms mingled
with the black juice of his barbed opponent.

                    Good God,
my mother said, and then
Where are your glasses?

She fetched
a cloth, warm water and iodine. We were dispatched
dramatically in the dark
to search with flashlights among the broken canes
to find the glint of glasses
and return in triumph to see

Our Father,
with his arms around my mother
in the kitchen's halo of light,
to hear him say,
I'm fifty-five my darling,
I'm almost old.

JULIE VAN GORDER

Cranberry Harvest

The cranberries hide low under bronze leaves.
Heinz, the manager,
floods the fields with Pitt River water,
hires blue machines to thrash the water,
forcing the berries to float and form
a dusky pink surface,
pelicans on a Kenyan lake.

Heinz leads his shareholders
along peat dykes to watch
turbanned grandfathers,
(once farmers, now chest-deep in water),
corrall the cranberries,
sweep them, long slow strokes,
onto a conveyor that rattles them high,
funnels them into crates on waiting trucks.

The fields, now blank lakes,
reflect the gray October sky.

The shareholders circle,
shake hands, give thanks.

MARTIN VANWOUDENBERG

The Beer Stein

so much depends
upon
the battered beer
stein

half empty
beside the salted
peanuts.

TREVOR CAROLAN

In November Light

A mile past Old Clayburn Road, on #11
a thousand swans flock the winter cornfield
white as a blessing.

A quarter hour ago, the waitress gave you a wink
at the diner, while young bucks prepped their snowshoes
for the high country.

We are stalled in traffic here, where rural starts running to wild,
ringed with dumplings too abrupt for mountains,
too large for hills, dark with forests that feed the shake-mills

along the river. Winter is beautiful, even in the aggravating days,
short of light, with the Abbey bells intoning across the heights
above Hatzic floodlands.

Late on their voyage south, the swans hunker down as
evening draws to darkness at five o'clock.
In their weariness they glean the muddy fields beyond

the fenceposts, while traffic moves on again toward the north.
And so we pass in deepening November, each to our hearths,
our migratory paths connecting briefly,

sojourners of earth and heaven,
temporal and eternal
down in the valley.

WALTER NEUFELD

Kroeker's Glory

Everything was ready to go. John's dad told him to bring the wheelbarrow over to Tante Tina's. When John asked why, his dad told him they were making hamburgers. John liked hamburgers.

Tante Tina lived with her three children across the street on a small farm. John visited often when he was little. He enjoyed being with her and she enjoyed him. She made him feel important. When she talked to John, she knelt and looked in his eyes. She showed him how to make a bull drool with mash and molasses; giggled when she squirted him with milk from the cow's teat; let him use a razor sharp knife to hack the stalk off beets he had pulled from the garden, and, when he cut himself with it, she swallowed him against her chest with her arms and as she cleaned and bandaged the bloody slash, told him, "Ahhh, there, it's not so bad, you're such a brave little workerman. I wish you were my son, then you could help me with the farm when I get old because I have no man." He believed her.

Her husband had died in a threshing accident in Russia, just after their second child was born in the Ukraine. She survived with the kind help of her neighbour, Franz Kroeker. Franz used to skitter to her house at dusk once a week, stooped over a bit of bread or potato. His own family had barely survived the winter of '44 by eating grass, and yet he brought her food. When nosy neighbours asked if he was the shadowy saint they had seen bringing food to Tante Tina at night, he solemnly denied it. They stayed suspicious because the mysterious "saint" had Kroeker's walk: a-kind-of-tripping-forward. No one else walked like that. Some of the villagers had even wondered out loud about "which end of his family potato" Franz had shared with her.

Ewald, Tante Tina's third child, was born shortly after she arrived in Canada.

John pushed the wheelbarrow, with a shovel, a long rope and pulley, to her house. It had been built in a grove of evergreens with huge trunks that reminded John of his aunt's legs. He looked up at the rustling branches, amazed. The bare ground under the trees was covered with a coarse blanket of rust-coloured needles. The air smelled fresh where he walked. Scrubbed clean. John heard crackling behind a tree and as he came round it, saw his dog hunched over a bone. The sound of it made him shiver.

His dad asked him to set the wheelbarrow next to the swing built between two trees, dig a hole in the garden and then go sit in the porch.

"Why?" he asked.

"Because I said so."

The porch was a short narrow room with windows on the south side to let the sun in. Potted flowers sat squished like parishioners on hard wood church benches set against each wall. He made room between two plants on the north bench so he could look out the window. From there, John could see his dad leading Kroeker the bull by a rope from the barn to the swing. Another rope was tied around its neck and then the two ropes were tied to opposite trees with Kroeker stuck between. John's dad took a .22 rifle out from behind a tree, placed the barrel between its eyes and pulled the trigger. Kroeker stretched out its neck and head, bellowed, then rocked back and forth. A long string of snot swung like a licorice icicle from its nostril. His dad reloaded and fired again. Needles sprayed out as the bull whumped to the ground. It gasped for air, belly puffed, *phuuuhh*, needles scattered at its nostrils, foam hemmed the rim of its mouth, and then its eyes waxed crescent white.

Kroeker's hind legs were trussed and hoisted up by the rope and pulley. The skin was cut, peeled off, folded and tied into a neat square. It began to drizzle just as the silver belly and intestines spilled into the wheelbarrow like swollen jellybeans. Ewald pushed the wheelbarrow to the garden. John noticed that he walked funny.

The ragged red, white and blue carcass swung lightly in the breeze.

Pee pooled in John's shoe.

Trudi Jarvis

The FraCan VI

Filtered through the leaves of the honey locusts, the early morning sun patterned Ann's room with a living mosaic. The waterfall and creek provided a constant background of natural melody, highlighted by the cries of Stellar jay, sparrow and robin. Freight trucks pulling into and out of Dad's truck stop across the Trans-Canada Highway added rumbling base notes. A CNR train sounded its whistle as it neared the trestle. The rhythms of Ann's days were established by the water, traffic and trains that flowed never-ending through the territory of her life.

Not thinking to tidy her blankets, Ann bounded out of bed, taking for granted that Mom would deal with the mess. She tossed her nightie on the floor, rummaged through her dresser and pulled on a bathing suit. She snuck downstairs carrying a happy face T-shirt and a pair of cutoffs. After using the bathroom, she put her hair in a ponytail and then grabbed some of Mom's cookies and an apple from the kitchen.

She sat on the back steps to tie up her canvas runners. The big old rose bush at the back porch had been planted when the house was built in 1955, just before she was born. Ann crept down the stairs and ate her cookies as she ran down the driveway. This was part of the Old Yale Road, the first road constructed between New Westminster and Yale. There was a clear section of the Old Road stretching for about half a mile from the back of the house through the woods to the railroad tracks. The Indians walked down there to cross the tracks and gain access to the Fraser River, where they put out their nets. On a hot day, they would sit in the back yard, trading fresh sockeye for cold beer.

The apple was gone before Ann reached the campground. Cedars and maples formed a solid canopy over the hard packed earth and picnic tables that made up Dad's camping area. She stopped for a drink, kneeling in the gravel and plunging her face in the creek. During high water at spring runoff and during the heavy rains in the fall, the creek would be brown with dirt. When the salmon were spawning, it would sparkle silver, almost congested with fish. Hunter Creek had many moods, all of them absorbed by the Fraser.

Ann ran to the river, branches slapping against her bare arms and legs. The sun had not yet burned off the dew, so she was damp and cool. She burst out of the trees into the CNR right-of-way and raced under the trestle, Hunter Creek glinting on her right. Plunging back into shade, she ran through the strip of forest bordering the river. The path ended abruptly at the edge of the sandy beach. Ann hit the end of the path at full speed and launched herself into the air to land six feet out and four feet lower than the path. She sped to her left along the edge of the clean water, beyond conscious thought, her whole fifteen year old being concentrated in the movements of her strong, muscular body. She ran effortlessly, aware of the sights and sounds of this incredible part of the world. The sky was clear, the mountains surrounded her, the creek flowed into the Fraser. The river was still slightly high and there was a calm pool of creek water backed up between the sandbar and the trestle. Beyond the sandbar, the Fraser flowed brown and strong. The tugboat shack floated in an eddy on the other side of the creek. These Fraser River tugboats weren't much larger than full sized pickup trucks. They were powered by huge diesel motors, had open exhaust stacks that could burn an unwary arm, had happily inadequate mufflers and displaced about four feet of water.

The tugs were busy this morning; two of them were collecting logs for the booming grounds. Both drivers blasted a hello on their air horns when they saw Ann. She waved back, splashing through a channel between the sandbar and the rocks. There were about three acres of water-smoothed mossy rocks beyond the beach, stretching to a point a quarter of a mile downstream. Ann's goal was the booms tied up on a straight stretch of riverbank just past the point.

There were two major logging companies operating in the Fraser Canyon. Together, they employed thousands of people, from fallers and chokermen to camp cooks and secretaries. They worked long, hard hours and were paid well. Logging only stopped for fire season and deep snow, both yearly factors in southwestern British Columbia. These were the last years of free-for-all clear-cut logging. These were the years before environmental protesters, before over-mechanization of the industry, before world wide concern over the old growth forests of western North America.

Rather than risk trucks and drivers to bring the timber out on the treacherous Fraser Canyon Highway, the logs were transported by water. They were dumped into the Fraser either singly or in bundles, each log stamped with the company's logo. A bundle consisted of an entire truckload of logs securely wrapped by heavy steel cables. Seven miles west of Hope, the logging companies had established their log catchment system at Hunter Creek. The small steel-hulled tugs were manned twenty-four hours a day. Two massive finbooms (chains of logs controlled by timbers spaced at right angles to the logs) were in place on either side of the River. One on the south shore could be winched to reach diagonally across the river; the other hung parallel to the north shore and directed the wood to the booming grounds at Ruby Creek. Here the logs were formed into huge rectangular booms, each containing maybe two hundred logs, depending on the size and length of the available wood. When the booms were completed, they were towed across the river and fastened to the south shore until the heavy tugs could tow them downstream to the mills and deep sea freighters in Vancouver.

Ann charged through the water to a small island of sand and snake grass. She tore along the island, invigorated when the stiff plants slashed her tanned legs. She jumped over the crumbling edge of the bank and laughed with joy. It was great to be healthy and strong, to be free to run in the sunshine, to be away from Dad's restaurant. If he had caught her, she would have spent the day cleaning tables, washing dishes, peeling potatoes and making French fries, one potato at a time.

Balancing on a log, she crossed a deep backwater to regain the shore. She ran along the steep bank, her feet never slipping on the wet, rounded, uneven stones. Reaching the point, Ann saw three booms tied up along the river bank, secured by thick cables anchored to big trees. She was able to jump from the rocks to the first boom with no trouble, knowing that the outside boomstick would not move. Straight sound logs were chosen as boomsticks, had holes drilled through both ends and were chained together to enclose the boom. Other sticks were laid across the boom when it was finished and were chained in place so that the logs could not shift when the boom was towed downstream.

Ann walked half the length of the boom, whistling with the birds, judging the logs. She knew the danger of this river, of what could happen if she misjudged one step and got pulled under the boom. Uncle Joe had been crushed in the booming grounds and had lost a leg. She now ran as fast as she could to her chosen spot, a big cedar halfway across the boom. Her feet touched each log so quickly that when one sank under her weight, she was safely onto the next. A fierce concentration possessed her; she was oblivious to everything except the wood and the water. She gained her seat and stretched out in the sun with her back against the central boomstick, exulting in her small victory, knowing that she could have crossed on the steady boomstick itself.

Ann released her hair from its ponytail to more thoroughly enjoy the wind. Sea gulls played on the river, landing upstream, floating down to a precise spot and then flying back to their starting place, over and over. Only one tug worked the river; the second was back at the shack. She closed her eyes. The water whispered its strength under the boom, birds cried their joy and the tug's big diesel purred in controlled power. The wind sent small waves lapping along the boom and tangled Ann's long brown hair. The only smell was of freshly cut trees: fir, pine, cedar, spruce and hemlock, all mingled in a perfume that would trigger memories of this place, this day, for the rest of her life.

The growing roar of an approaching tugboat broke her reverie. She watched as Uncle Joe drove the steel teeth on the front of the tug into the boomstick and laughed when he beckoned. She ran across the boom, not slowing to leap onto the narrow ledge around the tug's cabin. She gripped the bar mounted on the roof and was ready. Joe let the river pull his boat away from the boom and threw the throttle wide open, lifting the bow. The sounds and the wind caressing her body filled Ann's soul with elation.

Joe had worked on the river for over twenty years and was a master tug boat skipper. He knew Ann well and shared her joy of a perfect day. At full speed, he coaxed his boat, the FraCan VI, into his own Fraser River waltz, turning the steering wheel back and forth, back and forth. The tug rocked so deeply that Ann's feet dipped into the cold water. They were waltzing in the sunshine, in the clear air, in the water on a dance floor two miles long and a quarter mile wide. Their walls were mountains and their ceiling the infinite blue.

The dance ended when Joe slowed the tug and went back to work. He maneuvered the boat so that the teeth on the reinforced prow struck the end of a log. He pushed it across the river then gave a burst of speed to dip the log down and under the finboom, where it would float into the booming grounds. Joe whipped the tug around and raced upstream to get a bundle. Ann jumped down into the tiny cabin and yelled into

Joe's ear, asking if she could get the registration number from a small piece of wood somewhere on the bundle. He nodded toward a lifejacket. She put it on while Joe snugged the tug into the bundle and began the slow process of forcing the wood over to the north shore. Ann climbed out of the cab, walked around to the bow and jumped onto the bundle.

She stood on the highest log, part of all that was around her: the raw force of the Fraser River and the Coast Mountains, the power of the sun and the wind, the strength of the tug, the love of Uncle Joe. As the boat neared the shore, she looked down at the water rippling along the wood. There was something there – red plaid, bright orange suspenders, cloth tangled in the frayed end of the cable. It was a body – a man, a logger, dead and drowned in the Fraser.

Ann screamed high and long, loud enough for Joe to hear. She stumbled, her foot finally slipping, her body falling, rolling off the logs and into the water. Joe released the bundle and cut the engine. He limped out onto the deck, grabbed the long aluminum peevee pole, calling frantically for Ann. He spied her downstream, holding onto the fin-boom, fighting the pull of the current. The Fraser was so deep, so cold, the boom log slick and hard to hold. Ann was shocked, physically and emotionally, panicked at the memory of the huge sturgeon that Uncle Joe had caught here last fall. The river was bringing the tug towards her. Joe braced himself against the motor casing and extended the pole to Ann. She grabbed it and Joe pulled her onto the tug, led her into the cabin and sat her on the floor. He started the motor and eased past the bundle into the booming grounds. Ernie, the boss of Ruby Creek, brought his small boom bronc over and with both boats, they forced the bundle into a back eddy and secured it to the shore. Ernie wrapped Ann in his shirt and hugged her before Joe took her back to the shack. He phoned the police in Hope and then called the truck stop to tell Bill that his daughter needed him.

Joe and Ann were sitting on the bench on the shabby deck when Bill ran down the bank. He held Ann while Joe explained what had happened. Bill was not surprised that she had been on a bundle in the middle of the river. Drinking coffee laced with brandy helped Ann stop shaking before the police and the doctor arrived.

Alone in the tug shack, she watched Jim work while Joe took the men to the booming grounds. When Jim saw the body lying across the deck of the FraCan VI, he came back to the dock, tied up his boat and held Ann while she sobbed, out of control; as passionate in her grief as in her joy.

The dead logger, a family man from up the Canyon, was carried up the rocky bank to the doctor's blue station wagon. After Joe and Ann gave their statements, Bill and his daughter stood alone in the sunshine, reassessing the power of their world. White caps glistened in the water, tossed by the wind. The tugs danced in harmony with the timber floating down the Fraser. A train rumbled over the trestle, its whistle echoing over the valley.

Ann waved to Jim and Joe and grinned at her Dad. She kissed him and challenged him to a race home. She ran down the dock and dove into the river. Bill shook his head as he watched her swim, straight and strong and sure, toward her home and her family.

ALLAN BAILEY

A Pavane in Late Winter

Every morning he practised for five hours. He practised in his room in the small barn behind his family's house. He began to practise at about six o'clock in the morning. He started with finger exercises, went on to scales and set practise pieces, and then worked on longer pieces by Villa Lobos, Sor or Bach. His favourites were Bach.

He was nineteen and, like me, just out of school. He probably would have gone to university, but his family was poor, and even in Canada it is difficult for the children of the very poor to go to university.

His family were poor in a rural Canadian way. His father was a refugee from somewhere in eastern Europe. It was, they said, in Russia that his father's legs got ruined. Now an old man and a cripple, this father and his ever silent wife raised nine children in a decrepit farm-house that had once briefly been used to store hay. The Mennonite farmer who owned the house was a self-consciously Christian man, and he charged no rent.

This family, too, had once been Mennonite, until the old man converted to a more evangelical faith and took all his family with him. Although this apostasy perturbed many of their neighbours, they were not shunned by the people of the village; the Mennonites care for their lost sheep—they are a generous people.

The oldest daughter was an earnest girl, who lived in a tiny cottage a short walk away in the village of Yarrow, where she worked in the bank (that was before the bank building burned down and was never rebuilt). The second daughter helped her mother around the house. Randy, my friend, was the third child, and after him came six more. The youngest boy was five, and not in school yet. The old man, it seems, had remained active, despite his bad legs.

I suppose the family got some welfare money, and certainly the oldest daughter contributed to the family upkeep from her salary; rent was free; mother was thrifty. They were not destitute.

Randy had a bank account. He worked weekends in a gas station, and, of course, there was field work in the summer. He had saved over a thousand dollars, he had told me. That was a pretty sum in the early seventies. He still thought he might go to university.

Randy had fixed up a room in a corner of the barn behind their house. It was rough and uninsulated, but at least it offered privacy. I used to visit him there.

Although I visited him several times, I often think about my last visit with him. It was the day after one of those freak late-winter storms that suddenly and unexpectedly sweeps down upon our valley to dump a brief but thick layer of snow over purple crocuses or budding daffodils.

The sky hung low and grey that morning. The air was still cold, but the snow had stopped falling in the night. The snow lay everywhere, softly, like a hand on a friend's shoulder.

Mornings weighed heavily on my spirit in those days. After the world was gone off to work or school, I was left alone with little to occupy me but the weather, usually rain, and a pile of half-read books. So on that morning, as on many others, I had bundled myself up in my great black coat, bought at the Sally Anne for a paper buck, and set out to walk with no particular destination in mind. At least on that day, I could enjoy the diversion of the snow.

I did a lot of walking in those days. You might say that walking was my occupation. I had not much else to do: I had no television and no car. My rejection of possessions was, at least partly, philosophical. I had adopted a rather negative idealism. Cultural upheavals were rocking the world beyond our valley, and the ripples of those movements reached even to Yarrow. Besides, I could find no job. So I collected Unemployment Insurance, and lead a life of resigned leisure. In short, I had time on my hands.

I always enjoyed walking after a snowfall. I loved the muffled music made by the tires of cars passing on the snow-packed road. Some cars had chains that jingled like snow bells. Occasionally, bundles of snow fell from the branches of trees with a swish and a thump. Beyond roadside fences, the once-coarse winter fields now stretched out softened and transformed, as if thickly spread with fresh whipped cream, all white and yet-unspotted.

That morning, I walked first to the village, where I stopped at the post office for my mail—there wasn't any, of course—and then I decided to trudge out to Randy's place at the end of the mountain road for a visit. I dawdled, kicking up the snow with my workboots and throwing snowballs at telephone wires to try to knock the snow off them. The trip took me most of an hour.

From the road, I tread a fresh trail in the snow to the door of his room in the barn beyond the house. I could hear his music as I approached. I tapped lightly on the door, and he called me in.

I kicked the snow from my boots as I entered. The room was warm. In the middle of the room, a small tin stove crackled lazily. On the stove was a kettle steaming.

He broke off briefly from his practise to wave me in, but he didn't get up. I had come early, and he hadn't finished practising.

I hung my coat on a nail on the wall, and I left my boots making a puddle by the door. Then I went over and sat amongst the disarray of his cot, and prepared myself not to disturb him.

He told me he was working on a piece by Tarrega, and then he continued where he had left off.

I loved to watch his fingers dance among the strings, the right hand plucking and flexing deftly, the left rapidly stretching and contorting into impossible positions to reach proper frets. Usually, the fingers moved easily, habitually, but this was a new piece and they sometimes tripped. They picked themselves up quickly, and went over the same movement again and again until satisfied they had it. Then they continued on, confident again.

He was very serious, and he sat erect in an old oak chair that had once been painted, and then was scraped down to wood again, indifferently. His right foot rested on a wooden orange crate, and the guitar rested on his leg. In front of him on the floor, leaning against a table, a long mirror reflected back the image of his fingers in movement. His sheet music sat on a metal music stand to the side of the mirror. His brown eyes followed the music intently, darting furtive glances at the mirror. His jaw was fixed, but occasionally he grimaced as if, climbing a cliff, he were reaching for a hold and could find none. A thin moustache graced his upper lip. He wore a heavy-knit beige turtleneck sweater. His hair was slightly longer than mine, and sometimes his bangs fell across his eyes. Then a little flick of the head settled them out of the way again.

I waited.

I didn't mind the wait. I just sat cross-legged on the cot. I rested my chin on my knuckles. I probably looked the way a little boy does when he is allowed to watch his father perform some terribly difficult, terribly grown-up task, like polishing a shotgun or shaving.

I was getting a private concert, and I felt privileged. I admired my friend's seriousness—his sitting five hours every morning in a spartan room in a derelict barn in a small inconsequential town, practising his art.

Somehow it is easy to imagine an artistic genius living in a garret in Paris or some other great city. In our town, we had the genius but not the garret. I knew my friend was a genius—to this day, I still believe he was. But my feelings about genius were stronger then; now I'm not quite sure that I even know what it means, this word—genius.

When he finished the piece by Tarrega, I could tell that the practise was officially over. It was past eleven o'clock. But instead of putting away the guitar, he began playing a piece that I had once told him I liked. I remember that he had told me it was a pavane, and although I had no idea what that meant, I had been satisfied. Anyway, I knew that this extra piece was just for me because I was his friend. I felt happy that he would honour me thus. It made me feel closer to him—appreciated.

When he finished, he shook the hair out of his eyes, and then placed the guitar in the rich red velvet of its black case. It looked so beautiful resting there, like a princess in a coffin, waiting for the touch of her lover to bring her to life.

He was putting the mirror back on his dresser, and I said, "I like that last piece."

"I know," he said, "That's why I played it."

I was, somehow, surprised by this honesty.

Then he offered, "Tea?"

"Sure, sounds good."

He took out an old chipped tea pot and dropped in a pair of tea bags. He filled it half full with steaming water from the kettle. He stirred the bags quickly until they just began to colour the water, and then he deftly lifted them out with a spoon and tossed them into the woodbox. He took a pair of clear glass mugs from a little carved shelf and half-filled them with the brownish water. There was an open can of condensed milk on the table, but the holes were clotted over with a film, like yellow plastic. He scraped a fresh hole in the film with the handle of a spoon and then poured plentifully into the cups. The rusty-looking water turned the colour of pus. He dipped the wet spoon into a cut-glass sugar bowl and put two heaping spoonfuls in each cup. This sweet, murky mixture was what he called "tea." Although I hardly recognised it as such, I enjoyed it for the hot syrupy beverage it was. It warmed my fingers and my stomach, and left me feeling easy and content.

He sat down with his tea in an ancient, rather dilapidated stuffed easy chair that he had salvaged from somewhere and preserved despite attacks from mice and mildew. I almost lost sight of him when he first went down into this chair, despite my advantageous elevation on the cot, but he quickly resurfaced, head and shoulders above its wide worn arm. He set his cup to rest there after taking a careful sip of his "tea."

I wanted to talk about guitar—or rather, I wanted him to talk, as I knew almost nothing about guitars and had little to say on the subject. However, I was enthusiastic to listen.

I had some trouble turning him to the subject though.

He seemed to have had enough of guitar for the day so he steered the conversation onto religion by asking me what I thought about the Alan Watts book he had lent me. Then he told me he was reading somebody called J. Krishnamurti. I was always amazed by his ability to uncover new and, to me, obscure but brilliant and exciting writers with ideas that often caught me off guard.

He was soon telling me something about "understanding," and I was trying to follow his explanation. I was getting more entranced all the time when his lecture was abruptly interrupted by the sudden appearance of a cat that had all along been sitting just out of my sight in its basket behind the stove. The cat walked out onto the floor, stretched placidly, and then it moved over to Randy. It leapt onto his lap and lay down purring to be stroked.

"This cat is the best audience there is," Randy said, suddenly changing the topic back to music, "because he doesn't think about it. He doesn't know the difference between a scale or a symphony, but he sits there and listens from start to finish. He yawns. He licks himself. He watches my fingers like they were spiders. He is completely unself-conscious. And so he is never rude or pretentious."

"Yeah, but what is the use of playing for a cat? He doesn't know what is good or bad. He doesn't even know how difficult it is."

"That's right. So I never have to try to impress him, and I never have to fake it. All I have to do is play. Because he is honest, I can be honest. He brings out my best music. He just listens. He never judges."

"Well, then who judges. Doesn't somebody have to judge?"

"I judge. It is enough that I know how difficult it is."

"Then what is the use of having an audience at all then."

"Music is a kind of merging. That is what it is about. Usually, there is a composer, performers and an audience. But when it is really good, there is only the music. Everyone is lost in the music. It is a holy experience—outside of time and space. I play towards that ecstasy. I share it with the composer. But it is best when it involves a wider community. I need an audience. I need the cat."

"So play in the street for human beings. Play in a kindergarten."

"A kindergarten might be all right, but the big problem is ego. Ego and pretence. You can't be holy with ego and pretence. With a human audience you waste most of your music breaking down the ego and pretence. You only find a good space when the bored ones are asleep and everyone else forgets they are at a concert, sitting in their best clothes, listening to 'an up-and-coming talent'. Anyway, usually an audience won't even show up unless you are already famous, and there are only two really famous guitarist in the whole world today—Bream and Segovia. There is certainly nobody famous from this part of the world, and there isn't likely to be."

"So you play for cats?"

"Cats are fine people. They have no ego—or they are all ego, which amounts to the same thing. They certainly have no pretence. They are like little furry Buddhas."

Randy was my guru. I liked to hear him talk like that. I wanted to keep him going.

"Yeah, cats are happy little creatures, and cute, too. But what if it were a pig? I mean, a pig is a happy animal, and intelligent, too. But if I had to be a pig to be happy, then I'd rather be unhappy. Happiness is only a carrot on a stick, anyway. There are more noble sentiments. So would you play for a pig?" For some reason, I thought I was being profound.

Randy stroked the cat awhile. He pushed the hair out of his eyes.

"That's not the point. It is you that thinks a pig is less noble than a cat or a person. The pig and cat don't care. It is your problem. You think about things. They experience them. You think about music and performers and concerts. The animal just hears the music."

"So, Bach or a dog's fart—it is all the same to them."

"No, it is not. Music is special for every listening creature. Besides,

I play for you, too. Call it insurance."

Randy was my genius and my holy man, but when he had reached the end of some idea, I could never get him to do variations on the theme. So the conversation changed abruptly to poetry, and we talked about some poems he had just read by William Blake—well, he talked— and the room was warm, and the cat purred, and my tea went tepid in the cup.

Eventually, Randy suggested we have a bite to eat and then climb the mountain before the snow melted.

When we stepped outside, I could feel that it was warming. The clouds had risen, and the world had opened up a bit. Most of the snow on the barn roof had already melted, and from the roof, water dripped madly into a long spotted trench in the snow around the base of the barn. As we walked to the house, we left wet grey tracks behind us in the snow.

It was dark in the house when we entered, and I saw Randy's father standing in his crutches by the stairs. He looked very old and said something in German to Randy as I hung back in the doorway. Then he turned and slowly mounted the stairs on his wooden shafts. At each step, he seemed to waver as if he might fall backwards and tumble down the stairs like a bundle of loose sticks. But he made it safely to the top and was gone.

Randy's mother, a fat, quiet woman in a clean but well-stained apron, laid for us a small feast of various breads, jams, sausages and cakes, all made by herself. We drank deep from milky mugs of strong perked coffee. The kitchen smelled of spices and fresh baking.

Through the window, I could see the stark lines of an apple tree, and on a black branch, one withered apple still hung, a dark dab of sepia upon the mottled grey canvas of the late-winter sky.

We spoke little in the house. It seemed a place meant for stocking feet and whispers.

When we stepped again into the bright outdoors, I stopped on the porch to breathe deeply the fresh clean smell of the air. Together we walked to where the road dissolved at the foot of the mountain, just past the railroad tracks. Then we climbed the white path that struck steeply up the slope. The trail was slippery, and we had to bend low to grab bushes to keep from sliding back.

Soon we were breathing heavily, and our hot breaths puffed in the winterish air.

In a short time, we came out onto an old logging road, and our going was easier as we walked slowly up the mountain side. The road was seldom used, and along its edge, alder shoots pierced hip-high through the snow. We trudged along the open way, churning up the smooth snow.

I felt somehow guilty breaking up that pure surface with my boots, but then I noticed the lace-like patterns of the steps of smaller feet that had tread there before me. I stopped to study the pattern of prints stamped by some small bird on a smooth white surface. Randy stopped too, but there was nothing to say. We moved on together, climbing higher up the mountain.

Already we were hot. We were both wearing black wool great coats, and with our long hair and whiskers, looked like a couple of bears out of hibernation. We undid our coats as we walked. The snow was fast falling from trees all around us; the cedars, like gentle giants, dropped their white burdens to wave; a hemlock, slightly swaying on a little breeze, shook snow from green hair.

The road came out on the edge of a broad pasture. We climbed over a barbed wire fence and headed out over the white field.

The sun broke through the clouds, and in that moment, the whole world danced brightly around us. I began to run. I wound my tracks in a wide arch in the centre of the white pasture, circling in on myself like a crippled vessel on a sparkling sea.

Behind me followed Randy, moving steadily, thoughtfully, gracefully.

Where the field fell off steeply to a cliff, I stopped, and plopped myself down in the snow, panting. Randy came up and sat himself down beside me. Together we just sat there for a while and let the wet snow slowly soak through our great coats and trousers.

All around us, the world was quiet, except for the sounds of our own breathing, and the trickling of snow melting, and the occasional muffled thud of snow falling.

We looked out across the valley that lay silent and white below.

"Tomorrow, it will be gone," Randy said, finally. And we sat together, watching it go.

"What next?" I asked.

"I'm buying a guitar," he said, as if in answer to my question.

"You said you might."

"Yes," he said, "it's almost finished. I don't think I told you that. I hitched into the city yesterday to see it. I can get it in a few more days."

Somehow, I felt a little shock, and a little sadness. I didn't know why.

"I imagine it's beautiful," I said, as if he needed that support.

"It's lovely," he said. He looked a little sad, too.

"It will cost twelve hundred," he added.

It was hard enough for me to imagine having that kind of money, but it was impossible for me to imagine spending it on a musical instrument—a car maybe, a down payment on a house even, but I had never known anyone to spend any money on any art before—it just wasn't done in the world I grew up in. Money was made, and money was spent, and money was wasted, but it was never wasted on hand-made classical guitars. The idea shocked me somehow—it struck me as reckless and exciting, even a little dangerous.

"I'm still short," he said. "I'll have to sell my old guitar."

After a moment of silence, he added hesitantly, "I'd sell it to you for fifty." He spoke as if embarrassed by the of mention money between us.

"It's too cheap," I said.

"My father set the price. I told him I wanted to give you my guitar. He said, 'no'; he said giving it away would cheapen it. He thinks a musical instrument should be respected—you never give it away."

"Of course, I'll buy it," I said. I knew it was a fine instrument and worth much more than fifty dollars. It was a good deal. But fifty bucks took a big bite out of my "pokey", and I needed every penny of my government hand out to live on. I was already worrying about how I would spare the money—and for an instrument I could not even play.

"I would have given it to you," he added again, as if he were still debating the issue in his mind. He knew I was short of money, too. I knew he would give it to me then if I asked, but I just gathered a handful of damp snow and started to pat it into a ball.

"You can take it today," he said.

"That's okay, I can get it when you get your new one," I said. "I can give you the fifty tomorrow though."

"No. Take it." His voice was almost sharp.

I looked at him closely. His brow was furrowed, and he was staring into the snow at his feet.

Then he turned to me and smiled, and said, "You need to practise."

"I'm wet," I said, because I couldn't think of anything else to say. I felt as if there was something tragic in all this, but I couldn't say what it was.

"Yes, its good, isn't it," he said, and he fell back full length in the melting snow. So I did too—and it was good. We lay side by side in the wet snow, and then, like children, we each waved an outside arm in the snow. Then we stood up to see our "angel"—an angel with two bodies. And where we had lain, blades of green grass already breached the waning white surface.

"I'll keep it till you're famous," I said, "Then it'll be priceless."

He just laughed and tossed the hair out of his eyes. "Sure," he said, "let's just think of it as an investment in fame. It is just money in the bank." And he laughed again.

That afternoon, I carried the guitar home in its black coffin case. I set it in the narrow space between the foot of my bed and the wall of my room.

It was several weeks before I finally took it out of that case and tried to play it. All I could make were plunking sounds, random and aimless noises. The music was lost inside the guitar, and there was no way I could coax it out. I soon put it away again.

I guess I just had no talent for music because I never did learn how to play that guitar. I liked to look at it though, and hold it. It became my companion, and wherever I moved, I took it with me.

Years later, when I was living in Vancouver and going to university, the guitar was burgled from my apartment locker.

I missed it when it was gone.

I still remember looking at it, at the various grains of the wood, the delicacy of the inlay, the tautness of the strings. Every time I held it, I could recall the music that I had heard from it, and that I knew still lay within it. I knew the music was always in there, just waiting for the right strokes to tease it out.

For years after I had left Yarrow, seeing the guitar standing in the corner of my latest apartment or stored in the corner of someone's basement, I would always recall Randy, my friend, so soon disappeared from my life.

But it is gone now, and he is gone now, and I have never seen his name at any of the concert halls.

The years try to push his memory away from me. But Randy was my friend, and I always want to remember him, and the gift of his ideas, and the greatness I am sure he had—a greatness that was so clear for me to see within the little world we shared together, although it was lost upon the wider, more inelegant world without.

Sometimes, I wonder what became of him. But considering what little has become of me, in the end, I'm probably just as happy not to know. I cannot even imagine what he might look like now.

I would rather imagine him as a cat.

He has become a cat that wakes beside a crackling wood stove in a chamber made cosy in a corner of a cow shed.

The cat arches its back and stretches.

With nimble paws, it lifts, from out of her black coffin, a stiff and wooden maiden.

His touch gives her life.

She quivers.

They embrace, and then together they play music.

Together, for the entertainment of uncomely creatures, the dozing spider, the shivering mouse, they make lovely music, and with all that rapt barnyard throng become self-forgetting, and lose themselves among sonatas and mazurkas in the still dark hours of a chilly morning near a little town on the edge of nowhere, and at the very brink of spring.

Andreas Schroeder

Eating My Father's Island

I.

Letters like the one my father received on September 8, 1953, always caused consternation in our family.

For one thing, the address was typed, not hand-written. For another, the return address – BALLISTER, CLARKE, MARSHALL & ROBSON – was printed in gilt-colored ink. Only "the English" sent letters like that.

Our own mail, hand-scrawled and airmailed to Canada from Mennonite villages in West Prussia, always arrived at rigidly predetermined times – birthdays, weddings and anniversaries – and always contained the same things: a single-page report, an updated family snap, a bible verse and a pious exhortation. Letters from the English usually contained very formally typed documents with lots of heretofores and whereases and notwithstandings. Such letters almost always meant trouble.

That evening after milking, Father and I took the letter over to Onkel Jakob Sawatsky. Onkel Jakob was a short, fat man with a disproportionately large nose and a receding chin, both of which he'd tried to camouflage with a goatee and spectacles. He was rumored to be on a first-name basis with John Diefenbaker.

Onkel Jakob was publically ostracized but privately admired for his perplexing ability to make sense of heretofores and notwithstandings. His farm was a mess – just a sham of a farm really – with broken machinery and castoff junk cluttering the yard in a very un-Mennonite manner. His daughters danced around on his nose – everyone knew that – and his wife spent most of her life in bed (another decidedly un-Mennonite trait), so their garden was always choked with weeds and their herd records in disarray. In fact, most people visited the Sawatskys just to feel superior about their own neat farms – and, since they just happened to have them in their pockets, to have their English letters unpuzzled.

Onkel Jakob took Father and me to his "office" – a tiny windowless room off the kitchen that had once been a pantry, barely big enough for Father to sit and me to stand. The long pause that followed, as he gravely examined Father's letter, was probably the main thing Onkel Jakob lived for – those few moments when his social betters in the Mennonite community were obliged to acknowledge, however tacitly, his brief supremacy. Then he laid the letter on his desk with the appropriate gravity.

"So you entered a contest," he stated flatly, though not quite neutrally. Coming from any other relative that statement would have been unequivocally accusing. Entering a contest, a worldly contest, an *English* contest, had to be considered, for a Mennonite, very poor form. Not one of the Seven Deadly Sins, not enough to be mentioned from the pulpit on Sunday morning, but nevertheless, an undeniable instance of flawed judgment.

Father's face reddened. "I had to get Margarete's sewing machine fixed," he protested.

Even at my age – seven years and ten months – I knew that Father's embarrassment was really due to the fact that he'd been unable to fix the machine himself.

"And then he wanted me to fill out a …some sort of… paper for a contest," Father shrugged. "Something about an island – I can never understand the English when they jabber so fast. I wanted nothing to do with it, so he said he'd fill it out for me himself. What did he want with me and a contest, for heaven's sake? I'd already paid him for the repairs."

We all shrugged in unison, automatically. Who could understand the English? We were farmers, war refugees from Prussia, working ourselves to the bone to pay off our passage and the mortgage on the farm. The idea of an island was so incongruous, so absurd and utterly frivolous, it might as well have come from another planet.

Onkel Jakob frowned and refolded the letter like an Elder presenting the clincher in a scriptural dispute. "Well, but now you have the business," he said in a way that clearly meant: That's what comes from such thoughtless foolishness. "What has happened with this "Island in the Sun" contest, is that they've had a draw, and they drew your entry. You've won a prize – First Prize, this letter says.

"And First Prize, in this contest, is an island."

* * *

Onkel Jacob had promised not to tell anyone, and I'd only told my best friend Gerd and his cousin Willy, both of whom had sworn to keep their mouths shut, but within half a day the whole church knew about Father's island. I could tell because of the way all the men on the left and all the women on the right suddenly looked at us that Sunday as we walked up the aisle. Everybody was trying to decide how to react to this bizarre news. To a farming community like Agassiz, owning an island was either totally exotic or utterly silly – insofar as the two weren't exactly the same thing.

"Is it really true?" Tante Waltraut Doerkson burst out right after church – but safely beyond the church steps in the parking lot – "that you're going to give up your farm to go live with the English on an island??"

Onkel John, one of the eight John Klassens who lived on Edison Road and always gave their English postman nightmares, came up and congratulated Father on "winning Vancouver Island". Reverend Erich Friesen, in his gentle but firm way, took Father aside in the church foyer and reminded him that help was always available if he was experiencing any "undue spiritual turbulence".

We weren't sure ourselves what to make of the news. An island was obviously something the English prized highly – they wouldn't have made it a First Prize otherwise. But if it involved leisure time or vacations, it was decades too early for us. With our mortgages and CPR emigration debts, that was something we couldn't even think about, let alone aspire to. The only holidays the Mennonites ever talked about involved heaven.

Eventually Onkel Jacob offered to drive us out to Britannia Beach in his farm truck. That, according to his further enquiries, was approximately where our island was located. Today you can drive to Britannia Beach from Agassiz in less than three hours, cruising comfortably along a modern four-lane highway. In 1953 the journey took an entire day, struggling over two mountain passes on a single-lane gravel road, with Onkel Jacob, Mother and Father squeezed into the cab up front and the three kids – my two younger sisters and I – bouncing around on smelly barn blankets in the back. By the time we pulled into the first service sta-

tion on the outskirts of Baline Bay, eleven hours later, we needed everything they had to offer – gas, air, oil, water, toilet, tire repair and a fan
belt.

I don't know how all this was registering up front, but we kids were
absolutely goggle-eyed. At first it was just the smell – the mysterious,
slightly repulsive briny stench of approaching ocean. Then, a few turns
later, the stunning switch from landscape to seascape. All along the left
side of the highway, for miles in both directions, was rocky beach and
low surf; boats, log pilings, kelp-covered reefs, screeching gulls and an
open horizon that seemed to reach to the very edge of the world. My sisters had never seen such a thing.

"You like it?" Onkel Jacob grinned when we stopped at a marina
for directions. He waved at the scene as if he were personally responsible for the whole thing. "You must remember this from your passage,
Peter. Weren't you already five when your family came over?" He continued right on as if I hadn't nodded. "According to our Canadian
Citizenship instructor, this is the most island-studded stretch of the B.C.
coast."

"We own an island in the middle of … all those?" My 6-year-old
sister Gutrun, almost as tall as I and already in need of spectacles we
couldn't afford, was squinting hard at a string of large brush-covered
humps dotting the bay about half a mile offshore. In the late-afternoon
sun they seemed to hover in the gleaming water like herds of black-
backed whales immobilized in one of Father's photographs. Onkel Jacob
hoisted his birding glasses onto his nose.

"Those? Oh, I don't know about that. No no; I wouldn't think so.
I doubt that anyone would be giving away islands as big as those."

It took us another half hour to find Father's island. The directions
said 2.4 miles along Marine Road, starting from the B/A station – just
past its junction with McDonald Road. I knocked on the cab roof when
we passed the gravel road with its sign buried in blackberry bushes, but
Onkel Jacob hardly ever paid attention to kids so he had to turn around
about a mile later and go back. I knocked on the roof again as we passed
the junction a second time, but he didn't stop that time either. When he
finally did, after my third, really hard knock, he was peeved.

"What? You think *that's* McDonald Road? Come on, that's barely
more than a cattle trail. So then *that* … (he swung around, scanning the
boulder-strewn shore on the other side of the highway) … you mean

that would be the island??"

I guess I could see his point.

We were looking at a forlorn little pile of rocks about a quarter mile offshore, barely half an acre in size, with just a little fuzz of green on it. Through the birding glasses I made out some salal, that I mistook at the time for blueberry bushes, and a lot of bleached driftwood. No beach or obvious landing spots; just rocks and boulders around its entire circumference.

Father and Mother climbed out of the cab. "Na, have you two mariners found our Paradise already?" Father's forced jauntiness had already taken its cue from our obvious lack of enthusiasm. Mother looked ocean-ward with a carefully neutral face, shielding her eyes. Onkel Jacob frowned back over his shoulder, pretending to re-check the directions. "Just offshore at the junction of Marine and McDonald," he confirmed. "That looks to be her all right."

Father took the birding glasses and began a slow, methodical scan. Mother and I just looked, not saying anything. But my 5-year-old sister Heidi wasn't so careful about hiding her disappointment. "What?" she wailed. "That little thing? It's not even big enough for a heifer!"

"Well we weren't going to *farm* on it, you idiot," I sneered.

"Peter," Mother warned. Heidi stuck her thumbs in her ears and waggled her fingers at me behind Mother's back.

"Well did you really think the English were going to give you something for nothing?" Onkel Jacob laughed, an annoyed laugh that showed he hadn't been so sure himself, and now felt embarrassed about his lapse of cynicism. Only Father remained silent, still scanning the island.

"I don't know how we'd ever get onto it anyway," Gutrun grumbled resignedly. "We don't even own a boat." Having inherited a goodly dose of Father's practical nature, she suddenly saw a whole list of problems she'd conveniently ignored before. "And where would we get water to drink, anyway? You can't even really land on it; it hasn't got a beach or anything. And in a storm it would probably just go under water."

She climbed back onto the truck's deck and began yanking disconsolately at the scattered pile of barn blankets, while I wrestled with the bales that formed the deck's perimeter. Onkel Jacob walked around his truck clockwise and then anticlockwise, examining all the tires and straightening out his rear license plate.

"Heidi," Mother warned. "Stay on the road; I don't want you dirtying your school clothes in that ditch." She was wearing her second-best dress with the fancy stitching down the front, and both girls were wearing their good frocks and stockings. Even I'd been convinced to put on my green going-to-town shirt with the snap buttons and the two breast pockets. We'd all wanted to look good in Father's photograph of the family standing proudly in front of its new island.

Finally, Father lowered the birding glasses and handed them off to Mother. He zipped up his jacket and then cleared his throat in a way I've heard myself do at least a million times since.

"No," he said thoughtfully, rubbing his chin and gazing at the surrounding mountains in a manner already more proprietorial than tourist. "No, I don't think that would happen at all. You can see the high water mark quite clearly on the rocks all around the island."

* * *

It took a while for the true impact of Father's island to register on our lives – and that was largely because two conflicting assessments of its value began to circulate.

The first, probably originating with Onkel Jacob, held that the whole thing had turned out to be a low trick – just what you'd expect from the English. Father's island was just a worthless heap of rocks and bush.

The second, definitely originating with Onkel Jacob, resulted from his later conversation with Agassiz's only banker, Mr. Richmond Elliott Tunbridge.

Being manager of the Bank of Montreal, which held our mortgage, Mr. Tunbridge was most intrigued to hear of Father's island. It wasn't long before he'd informed himself about all its particulars. His eventual assessment, mentioned in confidence to Onkel Jacob, differed considerably from Onkel Jacob's initial impression. Mr. Tunbridge felt that while the island might not have a great deal of value just at present, it was bound to gain substantially from the extension of power and population into the Squamish Valley, which was expected to happen within the next decade or two. He saw it, therefore, as a "significant long-term investment".

Since Mr. Tunbridge was undeniably English, his grasp of financial matters could hardly be denied. Thus, the following conclusion evolved: The Canada Sewing Machine Company had tried to fob off onto Father what they considered a worthless pile of rocks and bush. But the joke had been on them. They hadn't counted on Mr. Tunbridge and urban development. Result: Mennonites 1, The English 0.

Being a pessimist, Father knew that safety lay more reliably in assessment number one, and I believe he truly tried to hold to that interpretation – especially since it provided him with fewer problems within the Mennonite community. In time, however, there were signs that he hadn't been able to keep at least trace amounts of assessment number two from seeping into his subconscious.

As befitted a man who had always kept his emotional life on a painfully short leash, these signs appeared initially as the subtlest of diminutions: a little less brooding, a little less bitterness, less tightfistedness. In time: a tiny bit more tolerance, a bit more equanimity, even a trace of hope.

I stumbled on dramatic evidence of the latter on the rainy Sunday afternoon following the delivery of the official land deed – in the hands of a photographer who'd insisted on photographing our entire family gathered around the sewing machine – when I heard a voice that sounded both like and unlike Mother murmuring something behind the closed door of our living-room. My thoughtless bursting in sent Mother scrambling hastily off Father's lap, her hair and composure in considerable disarray. "Na was?" Father protested, trying vainly to keep Mother from fleeing. "Just look at him; he's more embarrassed than we are! Hey come on, we're married for heaven sakes!"

In church too, Father greeted people a little less diffidently, stood and sat more confidently, and during the latter part of the sermon when he normally became fidgety, I saw him wide awake and preoccupied, scribbling busily into the margins of his church bulletin. They were just numbers – I snuck a look – but the upshot was that several days later, after another discreet and confidential conference with Onkel Jacob, the whole community – including Jacques Lafreniere, proprietor of "Honest Ron's Auto & Tractor Emporium", the only used-car dealership in Agassiz – knew that Father was seriously considering buying a car.

This was news to Father, who had merely been exploring the possibility of installing a used car engine into a burned out Massey-Harris tractor chassis he'd found jettisoned at the town dump. But the prompt and unctuous visit by Lafreniere, with hastily borrowed bible poking out of his jacket pocket, turned this unlikely idea into a more productive direction. Because in his eagerness to sell Father on the mostly imaginary virtues of a beat-up 1936 Chevrolet Town Sedan, Lafreniere said that she might not be so fast, she, and she might not be so pretty, bon, and hokay, de back seat she was missing and de back window she was gone, but sacrement and Mere de Christ, she was so solid-built, dat one, she could probablement tow a barn!

"Tow?" Father asked, turning to me. "What means 'tow'?"

"Ziehen," I explained. "Pull."

"Oui oui. Halage," Lafreniere encouraged, sensing an opening. "Drag. Haul. Hey, I even trow in a old trailer hitch."

"Why for do I want to pull my barn?" Father asked Lafreniere, genuinely puzzled.

"I don't saying you *want*, I just saying you *could*," Lafreniere explained, which somehow didn't clarify anything and undoubtedly became yet another entry in Father's growing file on the weirdness of the English – even when they were French.

But an idea had taken root, and while Lafreniere went home disappointed that day, Father was oddly thoughtful for about a week, after which he had a long talk with my Mother. Then, on the first available rainy day, Father walked all the way over to Onkel Jacob's farm, they both called on Mr. Richard Elliott Tunbridge, and an hour later Father bought the old sedan off Lafreniere's lot for $400 at $25 down and $5 per month – trailer hitch included.

According to Onkel Jacob, who was still shaking his head several weeks later, Father spent the largest part of his negotiations at the car lot lamenting the missing back seat, the missing back window, and the excessive amount of chrome on the sedan's bumpers – an excrescence self-evidently offensive to God, the Church and every right-thinking Christian. Lafreniere had finally solved this problem by dropping the price of the car by $50 and throwing in a can of black stove paint. "But you'll 'ave to paint 'er couple times a year, eh?" he warned. "Dat chrome dere, she won't take de paint so good."

For the next few days Father hauled in all the horse-drawn farm equipment he'd been promised for nothing by nearby neighbours, and modified the hitches to fit Lafreniere's hitch on the old sedan. He salvaged a set of winter chains from the garbage dump, and with these chains fitted to the sedan's rear wheels for more tractor-like traction, we were ready and champing at the bit for spring.

Incongruously hitched to a horse-mower, an ancient swather, a steel-wheeled hay wagon or even an antique 6-gang plough, the once elegant Town Sedan churned and skidded through our fields like a Marxist demonstration of the class struggle, its acres of chrome shining defiantly through thick layers of rust and mud. Father drove, while I stood in place of the conveniently missing back seat, my head sticking out of the conveniently missing back window, frantically pulling and pushing on the long levers as per Father's shouted instructions.

It took me a while to get the hang of it, and even then I could only move the heaviest teamster's levers with a mixture of panic and desperation, but with practise and more axle grease, we managed. "Getting better," Father said carefully after we'd mowed our first five-acre patch in the field closest to the house, from which Mother and the girls had waved and shouted continuously for the first half hour. "Try to set the cutter down a little earlier when we swing around in the corners."

I glowed at the way he'd said "we".

To everyone's amazement, the system actually worked. The car was virtually indestructible, and the farm machinery simple and solidly built. Parts, if needed, were always available in the weeds behind the manure piles of practically every farm in the Fraser Valley.

And on Sundays, for the drive to church in our very own car, I washed out the mud, pulled off the chains, and shoved in the wooden bench that Father had built. A bench that had been painted – it goes without saying – with black stove paint.

DAVID PHILLIP BENNETT

Mr. Yale and the Death of an Owyhee

"I think there will be fog by morning," James Murray Yale said.

"Oui ... it feels damp already, M. Yale."

"Another fall, another fog, eh, M. Allard."

Ovid Allard chuckled. "The fog makes everything damp and cold. I prefer the rain, or even snow." He pulled out his big key ring as Yale looked at his pocket watch. They watched setting sun, the people moving around Fort Langley's compound. Some of them were starting towards the big double wooden gates in the west wall.

Some of the people stood near the gates, watching the sun set. One of them was an Owyhee called Naole. The big Sandwich Islander looked lonely, staring through the fort's gateway towards where the sun rested on the horizon in a halo of pink and orange clouds. A thin fog was rising above Fraser's River. Thinking of home, Naole wondered what his family was doing. Perhaps he'd sneak away from this cold land and join the next ship heading for the islands with its load of salted salmon. He had yet to get an answer to his last letter, sent six months previously. Surely the Reverend Mr. Hammett had read it to his parents by now. He hoped there was nothing wrong at home, and the delay was merely because of the time it took for a ship to go to the islands and return.

An Indian woman paused as she passed him. Naole might be one of the lowest caste, but she found him attractive. She sidled up to him and slipped an arm around his waist.

"What do you want, Emilie Kwantlen?"

She smiled up at him. "You looked so alone, I thought you might like some company."

"You are Auguste Boyer's woman. You should be with him."

"Bah! August! ... I just want to be friends with you."

"That would be fine, if Auguste says it is. Have you asked him?"

"No, of course not. Besides, if I did, Auguste would hit me."

"And if you don't stop, he might hit both of us."

A jangling of keys came from the Big House at the top of the hill, and they heard Ovid Allard calling, "Sundown! All Indians out of the

116

fort. Sundown! All Indians out of the fort."

The few Indians still inside the fort's walls began streaming past them. One of them cocked an eye at Emilie and made a rude face as he passed.

She stuck her tongue out at him. "That one, he is silly," she whispered. "Not like Auguste."

"Why do you say that?" Naole asked, turning to walk inside the walls.

"He was to be my husband before August came along. He is still mad."

"Emilie! What are you doing with that low-life?" Auguste Boyer came charging down the slope from the bunkhouse, waving his fists, his short bandy legs pumping furiously. His open Hudson Bay blanket coat flapped behind him, the red, white, and black colours mixing in a blur.

"We are just talking, cherie."

"Well, you stay away from him, you hear, or you'll both answer to me!"

"Oh, bah! Can I not have a friendly conversation with a man without you getting jealous?"

"No! Not a man like that one anyway." He swung around on Naole. "You stay away from my wife, hear."

"I was not trying to be near your wife."

"Well, stay away, anyway." He grabbed Emilie's arm and yanked her away towards the bunkhouse.

"Auguste Boyer!" The reedy voice of Mr. Yale cut through the twilight like a willow switch. He stood on the porch of the Big House, waiting for Allard to return the keys, his black frock coat turned brown in the glow of the setting sun.

Boyer stopped in his tracks. "Oui, M. Yale?"

"You know my rule about mistreating wives, even country wives. I have heard tales of how you treat Emilie. If you want to stay here for the winter, I advise you to behave yourself. Otherwise ... it's back to Fort Vancouver with you."

"Oui, M. Yale." He released Emilie's arm and walked stiff-legged into the married personnel's bunkhouse.

Naole shook his big head and headed to the bachelor's quarters. He didn't like the short French-Canadian any more than the rest of the people did, and would hate to have a fight with him. The man's powerful arms and shoulders, developed from his years as a voyageur, could hurt a man easily. He sighed. Tomorrow would be another long day in the fields, digging potatoes.

* * *

The fog settled on everything, dripped from bare tree branches to the soggy ground and onto the heads of the Owyhee workers. Naole and the rest of the farm labourers squelched along the trail from the fort to the farmlands, their tools slung over their shoulders. He was the last in line, behind the others by some yards. He heard someone in hurry behind him. Trying to catch up, he thought. The rest of the crew disappeared around a bend in the trail. He heard a swish of air. He didn't live long enough to recognize the sound.

EXCERPTS FROM THE PRIVATE JOURNAL OF JAMES MURRAY YALE
Oct. 16th, 1848
Eliza says Aurelia and Isabella are doing well in their lessons. I wish I had more time to devote to my girls. Eliza has a bad cold. I hope the others don't get it. The Weather has been so cool and damp, it is a wonder we all are not sick.

I miss the council of my old friend Whattlekainum, but his Bones sit now in their cedar coffin in the tree across Fraser's River and I will see him no more.

I again had to remonstrate with Auguste Boyer. He has been beating his wife and acting the total Bully to anyone who approaches her. The Indian she was supposed to marry has been making trouble as well. Mr. Allard has separated him from Mr. Boyer twice in the last two days.

There has been no sign of the Owyhee, Naole, since Tuesday last. None of the Indians admit to taking him down river, nor do any of them confess to seeing him. He is a good worker and I don't want to lose him. The Owyhees don't know where he went either. We have not found his tools.

Oct. 21st, 1848

Auguste Boyer is becoming a severe Problem. Today he attacked two men who were seen talking to Emilie Kwantlen. These men were merely working in the same field with her. M. Boyer hit one very hard with his shovel and the man will be laid up for several days as a result.

There is still no word about Naole. I have sent word all up and down the river and down the Coast for the Indians to watch for him. I worry that he has tried to go overland to Fort Nisqually or Fort Vancouver to try and get a passage back to the Sandwich Islands. The other Owyhees say he has not been happy here and has not heard from his family for some time. The Clallams have been causing Trouble along that route again and he may have fallen afoul of them.

Oct. 31st, 1848
I have given up the search for Naole. Luckily most of the harvest is in now, so missing a man will not present much of a hardship. It will save the Company £17 if Naole has deserted, with our complement now down to 25 men.

* * *

Ovid Allard seldom walked the route to the farmland, but this day he had a message for the foreman. He took a childish delight in scuffling his feet through the fallen leaves and listening to the breeze rustling through the bare tree branches. Near the field he was heading for, he saw something glinting in a shaft of sunlight. He stepped off the trail and went to see what it was.

The metal end of a shovel protruded from a pile of loosened earth. Wondering how it came to be there, he bent to tug it out of the ground. There was a dark stain on one side of it, marking a small dent.

"Now who would be digging holes in the woods and leave a perfectly good shovel here?" he asked aloud.

It was an ordinary shovel with a long oaken handle, the same as dozens of others the farm labourers used. Curious about the digging, he started moving the loosened earth aside. After a few shovels full, the blade hit something solid. He cautiously scrapped aside some dirt, and saw cloth.

Naole had been found.

EXCERPT FROM THE PRIVATE JOURNAL OF JAMES MURRAY YALE
Nov. 20th, 1848

Ovid Allard this day found the remains of the Owyhee Naole. He has been murdered most foully and buried near one of the farm fields. Buried with him was one of the labourer's Shovels, which was apparently the murder weapon, for it has traces of blood on it, and a dent where it hit the man's head.

I have sent Emilie Kwantlen back to her people to heal. Mr. Boyer broke her arm yesterday. I am sending him back to Fort Vancouver in an effort to end is disruptions. Let Governor Simpson deal with him!

The last of the Indians who went up Fraser's River to fish have now returned to their camps at the coast. We have managed to trade for a goodly store of salmon, which the Men are smoking The hunter has brought in two more Red Deer and with the harvest from the Farm now brought in, we are well provisioned for the winter.

* * *

Ovid Allard stood in front of the men assembled before the Big House. He had separated the French-Canadians, Scots and Owyhees from the their country wives and the Indian workers. Standing restlessly, murmuring amongst themselves, they awaited Mr. Yale.

When he stepped onto the porch, he looked grim. He leaned on the railing and glared at the assembly for several moments before speaking.

"I'm sure you have all heard of the death of the Owyhee Naole ..."

One of the Indian women gasped and began wailing. He saw Auguste Boyer start from the group he was standing with. Allard waved him back. Several of the women surrounded her and gave comfort.

"He was murdered by some one of you by being beaten over the head with one of our shovels. I want to know who did it. If any of you have any information, please confide it in me, or in Mr. Allard as soon as possible, so we may see justice is done for this poor man.

"I will await in my room for anyone who wishes to speak to me.

Mr. Allard, you may dismiss the men."

In Yale's room, Allard sat by the desk. "I have been thinking about the shovel that killed Naole," he said."

"Yes?"

"It has a shorter handle than many of them."

"Yes?"

"I believe the man who used it to kill Naole was short. Perhaps one of the voyageurs."

"How would you find out which one?"

Allard shrugged. "I don't know. But we should be able to narrow the search by looking at the men and seeing what shovels they use. It would at least remove suspicion from some of them."

Yale nodded. "If nobody comes forward this day, in the morning, inspect the men and their tools."

The day dragged on into night with no word forthcoming.

Ovid Allard watched the men the following morning as they picked up their shovels from the tool shed. The tall Scots and the Owyhees selected longer handled ones, while those the French-Canadians selected were usually shorter. He mentally noted those shortest ones, three men. He wrote the names down in Yale's room, and handed the paper over.

After work that evening, Yale assembled the three men in his room. "I believe we have narrowed down to one of you three the man who murdered Naole," he said.

The men began remonstrating loudly. He waved them to silence. "I know only one of you is responsible. I have my suspicions which of you it is," he said, staring at Auguste Boyer, "but I have no proof. If none of you is willing to accept the blame, as a good Christian, then I shall be forced to send you all back to Fort Vancouver and let Governor Simpson handle it. Well?"

The men jostled and shouted, arms waving, faces red or pale.

Finally, Yale shouted, "Silence! M. Boyer is already being sent to Fort Vancouver. If none of you is willing to confess, or knows nothing to point to the guilty one, then you all shall go with him. Is that understood?"

"Good! Auguste Boyer said. "I would sooner spend the winter there than here anyway."

"You are a fool," one of the other men said. "There you will work twice as hard."

"Bah! Auguste Boyer is not afraid to work. He is not afraid of any man alive, either," he added, hand on his knife hilt.

"And what of your Emilie? Do you abandon her too?"

"There are women in Fort Vancouver too, mon ami. I will leave her to the Owyhees, since she seems to like them so much.

"Besides, she is no good with a broken arm."

EXCERPT FROM THE PRIVATE JOURNAL OF JAMES MURRAY YALE
Nov. 30th, 1848
Word reaching here from Fort Vancouver says that the party with which I sent the French-Canadians arrived without M. Boyer. He fought with one of the sailors on board the Maria and received a mortal wound. He was buried at sea near the mouth of the Quinault River.

Though it is cold this year, I don't think it will be as bad as last winter, the coldest we have record of ...

* * *

Emilie Kwantlen sat on a log, alone by the river, nursing her healing arm and her memories. Auguste Boyer was gone. Naole was gone. Snow drifted softly down onto her shoulders. She could hear the flakes rustling as they fell. She pulled the Hudson Bay blanket closer around her shoulders. Across the river, she could see a vague outline of Fort Langley, obscured by the snow.

She looked up, sensing a presence behind her.

"Come, be with me, as it was meant to be," the man said.

"Yes," she said, standing up.

Note: Ovid Allard and James Murray Yale and his daughters were real people, employed at the Hudson's Bay Company's Fort Langley in the 19th Century, as was the Kwantlen chief Whattlekainum. And there were many Hawaiians working for the Company. Everyone else, and the incident described, are fictional imaginings.

HELEN GRACE LESCHEID

Finding a Home in the Fraser Valley

A young widow from the Ukraine gathered her four children around her in the cramped room which had become their first home in Canada. It was really just a renovated porch which the kind Canadian farmer's wife had hurriedly readied for them.

That early evening in August 1949, the newly arrived immigrants had just eaten supper with their host family and helped put the dishes away. As evening shadows lengthened over the Manitoba prairie, cars had begun to arrive in the yard. Soon people with gift-wrapped parcels had entered the farm kitchen. It was for this reason that the young woman had hustled her children back into their room.

"These people are having a party and you are to stay out of the way," she told her children. "We will amuse ourselves right here. Understand?"

Suddenly the door burst open, framing the farmer's wife. "We would like you all to come to the living room now," she smiled.

"Us? Why?" the immigrant woman's face flushed in confusion.

"A shower-party for you," the farmer's wife announced matter-of-fact. Then putting an arm around the hesitant younger woman, she said, "Come, this is the way we welcome people into Canada."

As a 13 year-old girl who'd already experienced some of the brutality of life in war-torn Europe, I marvelled at such kindness. And I wondered what kind of a country this was, where total strangers make a welcoming party for you.

Finding a job became my mother's immediate concern. But in that isolated farming community, there was nothing for her to do. About that time, a letter arrived from her sister in Surrey, British Columbia. "The potato harvest is on right now," she wrote. "Farmers are asking for more farmhands. Why don't you come here? You'll have no trouble finding work." Soon we were on the train to the beautiful Fraser Valley. The day after we arrived on a farm on the Mud Bay flats between Cloverdale and White Rock, my mother joined the harvesting crew. The sun warmed her back as she dug her hands into the soft, black earth, and collected beautiful netted gems into a pail. *This feels like home*, she thought, *I will be happy here.*

From the first thaw in spring until hard frost in fall, my mother worked with the crew planting, weeding and harvesting vegetables for 50 cents an hour. During winter months she supplemented her income by cleaning houses. We older children helped out as well, mostly during summer vacations when seasonal workers were hired.

We were a motley crew on Matt Kennedy's farm: Chinese men and women with broad-brimmed hats chatting in singsong; Hungarian refugees trying hard to teach us younger girls some choice phrases; a Dutch, eligible bachelor who became our crew boss; even some bona fide Canadian women and young people.

We worked well together and often shared a good laugh. But they never laughed at my weird pronunciation of English words (even though I practiced for weeks to make the "th" sound soft, it still came out hard.) In other countries where I had lived, our differences had made us the brunt of jokes, but here I sensed genuine interest, not only in me, but in the other immigrants as well. *What makes Canadians so accepting?* I wondered.

Canada offered us other amenities which to my young mind seemed heavenly. As long as I could remember we had lived in just one room, sometimes sharing it with another family. Now we had a bedroom, kitchen, living room and bathroom-four rooms to ourselves! Ah yes, to separate my brother from us girls, my mother had put a cot into the bathroom, but still-so much space!

Big yellow school buses picked us up within a stone's throw from our house and, because primary and secondary education was free, each of us children could attend high school.

The day we became naturalized Canadians was a very proud day for us. Now my mother could vote and in a couple of years I would be able to vote as well. For displaced persons like us who had been shunted from country to country, the joy of finally belonging—of having a home country—was huge.

My mother coupled working for a living with domestic duties until the day she turned 65. Each of us children enjoyed post-secondary education. Sometimes I think I ought to have quit school and helped out financially, but my mother had dreams for each of us. In other countries where we'd lived, these dreams would have seemed preposterous, but here? With hard work and good management, her children might have a chance.

Over fifty years have passed since that first shower-party when we were so warmly welcomed into Canada. Since then my mother and I have seen many of our dreams realized. Each of us children has done well in our chosen professions of teaching and nursing. We have bought homes of our own and travelled and enjoyed so many of life's blessings in a free country.

I admit, much of the credit of our success goes to the spirit of my mother which she passed on to us. But still, had we remained in the Ukraine, would we have done as well? Would my children now realize their dreams? I think not.

And that is why when I see a Canadian Maple Leaf unfurled in the wind or hear the majestic sound of our Canadian anthem, my heart swells within me and tears come to my eyes. There is no better country. There are no finer people.

LESLIE J. BRYANT

Growing Up On The Farm In Rosedale

When I was about six or seven I was always outside doing things. In the springtime, me and the kid next door were gone on Saturday and Sunday to the bush, to Uncle Reg's collecting barberry bark to dry and sell for pocket money. Barberry/cascara bark, was in demand and processed as a laxative. At the same time we brought home lots of wild Easter Lilies (Trilliums) for Mother. In the fall time we tried to beat the squirrels to the wild hazel nuts. The squirrels mostly won.

By the time I was seven or eight I was into horses. I never did have my own bike and often got into trouble for borrowing Fred's, but I did have my own pony, which I enjoyed. I got the pony because I always had to chase the milk cows morning and night to the Stringer field, Castleman Road, or the Foster Place. At Old Yale and Bustin Roads, I had to chase the cows before school and as Dad and older brothers never got them milked too early I was often late for school. I would put my horse in the field across from the school and ride home for lunch, as Mom was often too busy to make my lunch in the morning. I always had lots of bumps and bruises from playing with the bigger kids or falling off horses. One that I remember was riding home for lunch and as I did not have shoes on my horse, I always rode on the side of the gravel road. This day I was in a hurry and going as fast as the pony would, when I came to Mrs. Martin's place that had lots of brush growing along the fence and there was a fellow talking to her over the fence. Just as I got there he stepped out and the horse must have jumped three feet side-ways and I was on the ground. I had to walk home and all the way to the backfield to catch my horse and I was late for school that time for sure.

When I was ten or twelve, I often stayed home from school to drive the horse three abreast on the discs. Because I was smaller than a man was, I was able to ride on the disc that had a seat on it. Dad and Donald did the plowing. We always tried to have three teams for the spring work but always seemed to be one or two horse short. Every spring a rancher in the Interior brought a rail car load of horses to Chilliwack to sell at Gibsons' Auction in downtown, just north of the five corners. I often got to go with Dad to the sales to buy another horse or two. It seemed like the mares and single horses were the cheapest and what we got most of the time. I usually got to lead them the seven miles home. Dad would follow along in the car for the first mile or two and if I was getting along okay, then I was on my own. I didn't often try riding them, as we did not know if they were broken to ride.

The trouble with buying a mare was that she was most likely to be with foal and we never knew when she might have her colt. One mare that we got that way was in foal and we worked her six days a week for three or four weeks to put in the crop. It was Saturday and we wanted to finish planting before Sunday and we worked until ten p.m. We put the horses in the stalls for the night and on Sunday morning I went to feed the horses and there was a colt running around the barn and the mare was still tied in the stall. Because we had worked her hard every day she did not show any signs of having a colt, but everything was fine. The colt grew up to be a real gentle horse. Because he was born in the barn he got to be called Barney. John Clegg ended up with him as he had a horse that was the same size and they made a good team. Another mare that I remember was a real good workhorse. She had a colt out in the back pasture. Now, I had driven this mare most of the spring and thought that she was very gentle, but when she had her colt she chased me right out of the field and wouldn't let me near the colt for two weeks.

When I was about ten or twelve we had contracts to supply four-foot wood to schools for winter heat. We had a woodlot on the end of Chilliwack Central Road a mile south of the farm. Dad used to hire men to cut cord wood and pile it in one-cord piles (4' x 4' x 8'). One man that cut wood lived in a cabin on the bush lot. He lived on eggs, 3 for breakfast and 3 for lunch and supper. By spring he had a mountain of eggshells outside his front door. A man on a good day would cut a cord. I think that the pay was dollar a cord. Donald and I and sometimes Dad, would take the team and wagon to the bush and haul the wood to the roadside on a small sleigh made out of birch runners with a tongue, about a cord at time. Then we would load it on the farm trucks and Donald would take it to the schools, Robertson, East Chilliwack, Cheam and Rosedale. We also hauled out telephone poles, shake and shingle bolts. Often when we did, the trail in the bush was too narrow for the team so we snaked them out with just one horse. I would ride the rose back and forth, with the harness on—not very comfortable—and someone would hook the poles on and off. We did this in the winter months.

Later in the year when the pasture ran out at home we would herd the milk cows down McGrath Road back and forth morning and night past the school. In the mornings I would leave my horse in the field and after school I would play until I saw Eric Atkin's bus go by to catch the four o'clock ferry. As I never had a watch, I knew then that it was time to take the cows home. Sometimes I would miss seeing the bus and was late getting them home. When the cows had to go to the Foster place I especially liked going on the weekends as I could watch the Rosedale teams play baseball, before I had to get the cows home.

A few years later, Dad sold some heifers to a rancher at Forest Grove, close to Clinton in the interior. Dad and Donald set out to deliver them in our old truck. In those days it would have been quite a trip. Somehow in the deal Dad came home with a buckskin pony for me. I guess the pony was seven or eight years old when I got him. The story was that he had been caught from a band of wild horses when he was two or three years old. The cowboy that trained and rode him sure did a good job because he was the first horse that I ever had that knew how to chase cows. Often I was amazed at what he could do. If an animal broke out of the bunch and ran back along a fence he would just take after it on his own and the moment he got his nose ahead of the cow he would turn right back on it. He would do this at full speed and many a time I never turned with him, I just went straight ahead and fell flat on my face. Even after awhile, when I knew that he was going to do it, it didn't help, I just kept going. That horse surely taught me a lot about chasing cows!

I attended Rural Youth Leadership School in 1948 at U.B.C., and it was there that I met Nell Nicklin, a fellow student from Duncan, Vancouver Island. We were married on June 3rd, 1949 and in November of 1950, moved to Aspen Grove.

Donald White

A Flood Of Memory

To describe to you the great flood of British Columbia's Fraser River Valley in the spring of 1948, I must take you on a journey back to a very different world. If, at times my memory falters or my facts are not quite correct, please bear with me for I have lived an eternity since those distant days.

Imagine a boy with the mind of a romantic twelve year old at odds with the risk-taking hormones of his actual sixteen years. My coming of age was during the Second World War and those of my ilk suffered the angst of missing a great adventure. We were almost, but not quite, a part of those glamorized battles as portrayed by the likes of Errol Flynn and Gary Cooper and all the other Hollywood soldiers who really won the war.

At the coming of the flood, I was, and had been since age twelve, a member of the Royal Canadian Army Cadets, Irish Fusiliers Battalion, a part of the Reserve Forces headquartered at the old horse stables. This was a huge post and beam, wooden building occupying a square city block, right at the west end of Georgia Street at the entrance to Vancouver's Stanley Park.

I suppose we cadets were what is now termed "wannabes", longing to be real soldiers yet not quite old enough. I wanted to be, badly enough, over those four years, to attain the rank of First Lieutenant. Now as a cadet, I was given the amazing chance to skip school and go off to "fight the flood". At last, a chance to actually do battle!

It had rained a lot over the last two weeks and it was really coming down that afternoon as we prepared to board the big army truck that was to transport us to the flood. We cadets, being the lowest priority of the cash-starved armed forces, were not supplied with rain gear and had only our woolen khaki uniforms to protect us from the downpour.

At that moment I made a decision, ultimately changing the course of my life. Having spent the last two summers working in a logging camp on Vancouver island, (yes, in those days twelve and thirteen year old boys could and did find jobs, real work, during school breaks), I had acquired that essential for survival in the soggy rain forest—a genuine "Dri-Bac" jacket. This was a wondrous creation of heavy, waterproof khaki canvas crafted by the Jones Tent and Awning Company of Vancouver and a crucial piece of equipment for loggers.

I was about one hour, by bus, from my home in North Vancouver and I figured that I had time to get there, pick up my Dri-Bac, and catch my unit at Port Moody, where we were to load more cadets and equipment. I hopped off the truck and after a ten minute wait outside the barracks, I caught a bus to North Vancouver. Over the Lion's Gate Bridge and home took about another half hour. There I picked up my rain gear and with a quick goodbye to my grandparents, I boarded a bus headed for Port Moody. At this point, things started to go wrong. We came to a dead stop in a long line of traffic. There was some kind of accident ahead and we were delayed almost an hour before resuming our way.

When I finally arrived at the staging area I was greeted by a huge empty parking lot. There was nothing there but the rain falling and splashing in the puddles of that lonely place. After walking in circles for some time, cursing my fate, I gratefully found another human being, a passerby, an elderly gentleman out for a walk.

"Sonny", he said, "If you're lookin' for them other soldiers, they all got on trucks and left about an hour ago."

What to do now? Okay, head east. I'm bound to catch up to them sooner or later, right?

Oh yeah? I stepped out on the highway and stuck out my thumb. The first vehicle to appear screeched to a halt. Remember, those were different times and everyone picked up hitch hikers, especially someone in uniform. After several rides, just as dusk was falling, we drove into the little town of Maple Ridge and spotting a sign reading, Flood Control Headquarters; I asked to be dropped off.

I had arrived at the Community Center and before I could gather my wits, a harried looking person rushed up to me and shouted, "You were sent here by the Army, right? We need a sand bag crew, quick, out by the Harris' farm! 'Dykes starting to crumble!"

In a flash, I was aboard a flat bed truck, loaded with civilians, racing into the gathering darkness. Moments later, we slid to a halt at a scene illuminated by tractor lights. There was a man I surmised to be farmer Harris, standing on the dyke in the swirling rain, beckoning urgently to us.

When we reached him, he grabbed me by the shoulder and said, "Hurry! She's real soft here. She could go any minute!"

Only then did it dawn on me that I had been mistaken for a real army officer. Because of my Dri-Bac jacket, my cadet insignia was obscured. These people expected me to take charge of the situation. Fortunately, others in the group had experienced this present crisis and without a word everyone ran to a near by pile of sand, grabbed sand bags and shovels from another stack and began rapidly filling the bags.

"Over here! Right there!" cried Mr. Harris, still clutching my arm and shoving me to a spot on the dyke.

She was indeed "real soft" and felt like Jello under my feet. By this time a line of people had formed between me and the pile of sand and the first full sand bag was thrust into my hands. I threw it onto the mushiness at my feet and another was immediately handed me. The following hours passed in a blur. I remember the throbbing power of the river racing by , the inadequate feel of the queasy ground under me and the endless sand bags that I threw down.

Dawn broke, finally, to find our group exhausted but standing upon a much more solid footing. Hundreds of bags now reinforced the weakness in the dyke and farmer Harris, with tears in his eyes, shook my hand and declared, "You did it men, she's gonna hold."

With that, we stumbled to our truck and soon were back at the community hall. There, local farm wives had prepared a huge breakfast which I ate ravenously, then staggered to a line of mattresses in one corner and crashed into deep, wonderful sleep.

After what seemed only moments, I was shaken awake, a bag of sandwiches and fruit pie was shoved into my hand and we were off again to fight the flood. Another farm, another dyke, but this time we were greeted by, not the farmer alone, but two comely girls around my own age.

Here was a totally different situation from the previous evening. It was now full daylight and I could see the swift moving, muddy water rumbling ominously and carrying masses of debris; whole trees and parts of buildings. This was not to be a repeat of last night's triumph. Water was pouring over parts of this farm's dykes. We were here to help evacuate. Once more, because of my uniform, it was assumed that I was in charge, and again all seemed to know what to do and so I did not really have to make important decisions.

People were arriving from neighboring farms with trucks, tractors and horse drawn wagons and they started to swiftly load up the livestock to be transported to their nearby barns.

Partly because I was a city boy and insecure around large animals but mostly, I confess, because the lovely daughters were at the farmhouse, I took charge of loading furniture. Or so it seemed. The person really in charge, the farmer's wife, managed, in spite of the harrowing situation, to keep a wary eye on the daughters and myself.

We worked at a furious pace and the water pouring through the, by this time, almost transparent dyke was soon up to our knees and flowing into the basement windows of the house. The only good news? The rain stopped for the first time in days and the early morning sun shone gloriously through the clouds like a rescuer breaking down the door. This was not at all a welcome situation for me, however. The rapidly rising torrent meant that I, the person assumed to be in command, would, imminently have to order us out of there or all would be in serious jeopardy. Also, I was by now sweating profusely in my Dri-Bac. If I removed my coat, as everyone else was doing, I would stand revealed to these wonderful, courageous people as the imposter I was. The cadet insignia on my tunic would reveal me as a fraud.

Once again fate intervened and bought me some more time to continue in my role as a young army officer bravely at war with the forces of nature. "That's about it boys. All my livestock's loaded and it won't hold much longer. We'll have to leave what's still in the house. We better get out of here, right Lieutenant?" This last was addressed to me by the farmer. "Okay. Load up and move 'em out!", I shouted in a voice of command. I was falling ever deeper into my part..

The lady of the farm and her daughters gathered around me and with a group hug, declared "Thank you for all you and your crew have done. We'll be staying at the Brody's in town and the girls will be helping out at the hall."

As we parted, the oldest and prettiest daughter gave me a tearful smile which, to my youthful imagination, promised wonderful things to come. But this was no time for romantic daydreams. It was load up, sand bag, grab some delicious food, load up again, more sand bagging , sleep for a few hours and out again over, and over, and over until the line between waking and sleeping blurred and I could not tell the difference.

After that first day and night, I have to admit to becoming an active deceiver. I relished being treated as an adult and a respected leader. To my shame, I hid my telltale tunic at the bottom of my pack and, for all anyone knew, I was Lieutenant White, flood warrior extraordinaire!

As the days and then the weeks flowed by I believe I actually became good at my work. At least the grateful farm people seemed to indicate such by their acceptance, and yes, even admiration. During this time we had our victories and our defeats in the great war against the mighty Fraser River but there were no human casualties save one boy who fell off a truck, breaking his leg. This euphoric diorama would soon change for me with the arrival of the Royal Canadian Navy. I was about to experience my first real failure in battle.

I awoke from a marvelous dream of farmer's daughters to find the dispatcher shaking me and shouting, "Quick! You've got to take a crew down to the landing. Barnston Island's about to go under and the Navy is here with a barge. C'mon, move it!"

Oh, no, the Navy? My sinking stomach told me I was in deep trouble. For the past two weeks I had been knowingly impersonating an officer. Don't forget that this was the era when such offences were taken very seriously. I rapidly threw on my trusty Dri-Bac and attempting to gather my widely strewn wits, I hurried to a waiting truck and was whisked all too rapidly towards my impending doom.

When we arrived at the landing, not really such anymore, as the wharf was underwater, I saw, moored to a post still jutting above the swollen tide, a large, blocky Navy Landing Barge. As we approached to board her, I ascertained that she was manned by two sailors and an officer, a dark haired, neatly bearded young gentleman of somewhat stern appearance, who was standing in the bow.

"Get aboard, quick." he cried, "Barnston's Dykes are mush and they're liable to go anytime. That island's way below river level but we'll try and save her."

He turned to me as our sand bagging crew started aboard. "I'm Lieutenant Breton." he stated, eyeing my quasi-military uniform, "And you are?"

"I, aah, um, Don." I replied, with truly amazing repartee.

"Don, huh? Okay, hmmm. The people at the landing here tell me you've been doing a pretty good job. Well, get on board. We've no time to waste." With that, he took the helm, and with a shout of , "Cast off,

Seaman." We were launched upon the angry water.

Luckily for me, it was a grey, stormy morning, and so I was safe in my disguise behind my Dri-Bac; or so I thought.

The voyage out to Barnston island was tense, what with dodging floating debris and fighting the turbulent currents and eddies of the murky river. The throbbing rhythm of the powerful diesel engine seemed to now and then miss a beat, causing a shot of adrenaline to jolt me out of my imagined pending court martial for impersonating an officer. We soon approached our destination, a small island, looking to me to be about a mile long and maybe half as wide, dotted with houses and barns standing in partially flooded fields. Behind a thin dyke it seemed all to be below the level of the mighty river, reminding me of a saucer floating precariously in a pan of water. Could, as with the saucer, the slightest disturbance, sink it?

There was little time to dwell on these thoughts as we quickly land-ed at the first available mooring. Immediately we set to work, furiously sand bagging an ever soggier dyke. Remember, the dykes of 1948 were not of rock and concrete but were merely packed earth mounds, held together by the roots of the grass that flourished upon them. Once the earth within was saturated they became mushy and weak. In spite of our Herculean efforts, the river seemed to gain strength and suck away, bit by bit, pieces of the insubstantial ground beneath us. We were all in dire peril.

At last Lieutenant Breton was forced to make the decision to take us out of harm's way. "All right, all aboard." he commanded, "We'll cir-cle the island and take on any civilians still here, so move it. It looks like we've no time to lose!"

Once again the powerful diesel pulled us into the torrent. We cir-cled the island and here and there picked up small groups. Lieutenant Breton was adamant about personal belongings or anything else to be carried aboard. There was room on the barge only for the people them-selves, or so it was hoped. We made a complete circuit and approached and prepared to board the final passengers. The situation as we fought the current in order to make a landing was becoming very dangerous. The river was now rushing over the flimsy dyke and pouring across the island!

As our prow nosed into one of the last remaining pieces of solid land, and the noise of the engine ceased, our ears were assaulted by a cacophony of screams. For a moment I was completely disoriented. What was that incredible noise? Then it became clear. There were a man and two young boys standing by a wagon containing about a dozen panic stricken pigs which were milling about and shrieking like the banshees of Hell.

"You gotta take my pigs offa' here!" shouted the man running towards our already crowded barge, "I can't leave em' to drown!"

Lieutenant Breton would have none of that. "Just you and the two boys, no possessions, and move it, this whole place is going under!" he shouted.

"I ain't go'in nowhere without my pigs!" declared the obviously desperate farmer. "Take the boys, but I'm staying."

Myself, I was at an impasse. What could we do? I sympathized with the farmer; the loss of his livestock no doubt meant financial ruin but there was no room for the pigs and precious little time to argue the point. Then Lieutenant Breton took decisive command. He quickly pulled his sidearm from the holster at his side, a forty-five which, to my wondering eyes, looked as big as a cannon and pointing it at the farmer's head, declared in the flattest of tones, "You will board now, Sir!"

But the man didn't buy it. "No way. My pigs go or I don't."

Obviously, he knew the officer would not shoot him. What could Breton do? Whatever, it was would have to be quick. There was precious little time, or island, left!

In a few strides, the Lieutenant reached the wagon and pointed his pistol at one of the screaming pigs. "If you move fast, you and the boys can get them off the wagon. Then they'll have a chance to swim for it. Other wise, I'm shooting them all, right now! They're not boarding this ship, but you and the boys are. Understand?"

There was no doubt the grief stricken man and the rest of us understood. Quickly he and the two boys and a few of the others on board unloaded the pigs and we were soon powering away from the stricken island.

I have often pondered the fate of those pigs but I have never doubted Lieutenant. Breton's decision. During our journey back to the landing, I reflected on my role over the past few weeks. What if, in my vain impersonation, I had faced similar responsibilities and decisions such as I had just witnessed? How would I have handled that kind of situation? I felt consumed with guilt and prepared to confess all and put myself at the mercy of a court martial.

The barge moored at the same pole where I had first encountered it and all too soon emptied passengers and I was alone with Lieutenant Breton and his two crewmen.

As I approached him in total surrender, a big grin came over his face. "Kid," he said, "I don't know who you are, or what game you're playing but as far as I'm concerned, you're playing it damned well. Now get off this vessel and on about your business and don't let me see you again."

These are my reflections on the great flood of '48 and of some of my first real skirmishes on the battlefield of youth. I can't help but wonder, as I recall those events of an, oh so different time, how they would play out in today's world?

MAY LA CHANCE

A Vacation in The Hop Fields of Chilliwack

In the late summer of 1940, families in the Fraser Valley took their children in hop season and picked hops while living in the cabins provided by the field owners.

After my father and brother took turns cranking the motor to the McLaughlin-Buick, we were off on our summer adventure. From Port Kells in the extreme northeast corner of Surrey, we traveled along the Latimer Road (192) to the Trans-Canada Highway (Fraser Highway) to Chilliwack. This main Highway was made up of sections of smooth cement. The neglect and poverty of the times was evident wherever you looked. The Highway had potholes and cracks, but there was a rhythm as the wheels rode over each join in that cement highway: I can still hear that *clicketty-clack, clicketty clack* as the car rolled over those perfectly proportioned cement blocks.

That McLaughlin-Buick was packed with food, clothing, bedding, utensils and other necessities to keep the family going for a working vacation in the hop fields. Nine people were packed into that well-built car: mother, father, four girls and three boys. The oldest child was a teen boy and the youngest twin boys.

In my memory, now six decades later, the hop fields were a geometric beauty, and free world of nature. Tall half-A-frame supports held up the rich cone laden vines. Rising twenty feet into the sky, everything seemed oversized, the long wide rows were evenly spaced and in contrast to the gigantic thimble shaped baskets. These three foot containers sat in those wide aisles waiting to be filled with soft green cones, and I was dwarfed below those mysteriously shaped baskets. Now, I guess that the open mouth was about two feet across. It must have been easier to walk a thimble shape along the soil than any other shape than any other shape of containers. Those wicker baskets were too heavy to lift, so giving them their own walking feet seems quite likely.

The hop fields and their harvest are a lasting memory which I can bring to surface at will. The yeasty, beer-like fragrance of the cones would fill the air. Evidence of the harvesting was left behind on the hands of the pickers in the form of dark green and yellow stains. This stain was as a result of palming clusters and removing them with the fingers. By the end of the day, the pickers' fingers were sticky, smelly, and stained. The hops look like a mini green cone, but feel soft and furry like a bumblebee or caterpillar. Although varying in size like green grapes, any one cone could fit nicely into my palm at three years old. While adult hands busied themselves in the hot August sun, the youth found ways to alleviate the monotony of picking hops. Socializing, flirting and exchanging ideas were a few of the ways to get through the hot August days, and many romances had their origins in those dusty fields. Dust and the bitter flavour of the hops would intermingle on moist lips. The hop cone was very bitter to my taste: at three years old everything must be tasted to be appreciated.

For families, the harvest was a means to earn some money during the beginnings of World War II. Getting away from the regular routine had been going on during the Depression and just continued on when war broke out. A young Navy man in his white shirt and bell-bottoms cradled his chin in palms while resting elbows on the rim of the mysterious picker's basket. The charming sailor was likely expending energy entertaining young ladies. It is only fair to say of the young people that they did go to the hop fields to earn money and give it their best shot for a small remuneration.

The giant wooden supports with wire runners held the fruit laden vines high in the air. There was a shade cast by the vines but it was not all that refreshing because the air stood still in those long wide aisles. The odour of millions of hop cones heating up, combined with the moisture around the roots of the vine was a stifling combination.

The general appearance of the area and fields was of a happy peaceful place. The open fields sat under a beautiful sky and were encircled by mountain ranges. The mountains were just far enough away to give a feeling of protection without closing us in. The silence of freedom in a warring world was cherished by all. Freedom also came by way of not having to wear polite street-clothing, or suffer the restraints of the school room. There was minimal discipline in the open fields. It was a vacation for us from small overcrowded houses: the hop harvest shut out the decay of life brought on by the ten year Depression, and now WWII.

Hopping around under the rim of the wicker thimble basket, I managed to say cool in my cotton dress. I watched the men and boys on A-frame ladders pick the upper vines. The teens below flirted with one another. Not far away was the boardwalk leading to the pickers' cabins. The cabins were bunkhouses with family rooms, about twelve feet by fifteen feet, of unpainted wood. Inside there were a few cupboards, counters, a wooden table with chairs or benches. Most important, wooden frames attached to the walls became bunks to lay our bedding on. I do not recall cooking stoves. In any case, our family cooked on a Coleman stove. There was no electricity in the cabins but that was no problem because everyone went to bed before sunset and arose with the sunup. The 'facility' was an outdoor community affair. For convenience, small children had Jerry pots under their bunks at night. Our water supply came from a community barrel at the entrance to the bunkhouse, elevated at the start of the boardwalk. Everyday, the supply man came with his horse and wagon and re-stocked our water and took away garbage created by pickers. This was a well-run little community.

In this setting, with families sharing the care of small children, I became the target of two naughty boys. Watching my mother pick hop cones, I stood beneath the rim of the thimble basket. An eight year old boy and his younger brother coaxed me away out of sight of watchful eyes. Now beneath the community water barrel, the oldest of the boys said, "Pull the plug on the barrel."

I looked at the boy. I wanted to play. "Like this!" he said. He pulled the plug on the water barrel nearly out but it still held back the water. Once again, the naughty boy said, "Pull the plug. Like this." With those words he pulled the plug to a 45 degree angle and the water ran out. He jumped back laughing and ran with his brother behind some long buildings likely used for storing or drying the hop corns.

While I was looking in the direction that the boys had hidden, an angry man came from behind yelling, "You let that water out. You let that water out!"

On hearing all the commotion, my father appeared and spoke much more wisely than the angry yelling man. "Where there's mischief, there's always boys."

"Boys," I repeated and pointed in the direction they were hiding.

"Did boys do this? Pull this plug?" my father asked.

I nodded yes: "Boys", and again pointed in the direction that the boys had last been seen.

The angry man insisted, "The little girl did it. She was the only one here when I got here." He explained. To eternity, this man insisted, "The little girl did it."

My father picked up my hand, set it across his palm and pointed out the frailty of my small hand. He showed it did not have the span to grasp the large plug; it did not have the strength required to pull the plug; and, he added, she does not have the reach to tug out the plug. "Look at that hand! That is not the hand that pulled the plug. It is physically not possible for my daughter to have pulled it from the water barrel. Find those boys, and you will have your culprits," he said.

In agreement with what I heard, I nodded and repeated, "Boys." Later I learned that the Star brothers were the culprits, but I lacked the ability to identify them verbally.

Now that I live in Chilliwack, the hop fields are gone and I have only pictures of the last fields before they were removed a few years ago.

ALVIN G. ENS

Entrepreneurship

We moved to this little acreage north of town for our sons, though I admit the farm boy within me welcomed a bit more land than a city lot. It's marginal farm land, overgrown with alders, cottonwoods, the occasional cedar, and some blackberry brambles. Here I delivered on my promise of a dog and a tree house. We even bought an ATV and cut a trail through the scrub brush.

That's when I discovered the western end of the property had a depth of good soil. And that's when I thought my boys needed a project to teach them entrepreneurship. I remembered my own glorious past of growing up on the farm where I learned to work doing chores and helping with farm projects. I even had some of my own projects—raising a few chickens, nursing the runt piglet and planting potatoes—being allowed the profits from my entrepreneurship. I suggested to my wife that the soil would be good for raising corn.

"In the wilderness?" asked my wife. "And who's going to find the time?"

It was enough to pique me into proving it could be done. I answered, "The boys need to learn the dignity of physical labour. Besides, that 1.8 acres is too precious just to sit idle. In fact, I hear that if you make enough gross profit on an acreage, you can classify it as a farm and pay a lot less in taxes. I'll help the boys get started. It could be a fine family project."

"Not family," replied my wife, "better call it a male enterprise with the possibility of male bonding."

I broached it to Jim and Ted after supper. "This Chilliwack Jubilee corn is really delicious. Maybe next year we could grow our own. What we don't eat you boys could sell at a roadside stand. You could probably supply the whole neighbourhood."

Jim responded slowly, "Dad, did you say 'we' or 'you'?" Perceptive son, that Jim, he'll make a fine lawyer some day.

I countered with, "I'll help you get started but pretty soon you'll be able to handle this project all by yourself. A little planting, a little weeding, a little harvesting, a little selling. Why, before long, you'll want to have the profits all to yourself. It'll be a good experience in agriculture, management, business, finance, entrepreneurship."

"Dad, if you want to keep us out of trouble, could you help us cut another trail for the ATV?"

"Always keep your eyes open for a good opportunity to make a bit of ready cash," I philosophized.

That fall we did double duty in land clearing. We prepared a stretch next to the fence for corn and cut a buffer next to it for the ATV trail. Jim entered in beautifully and Ted learned to carry and pile in little spurts of fitful activity before venturing off for washroom or snack breaks. And in good entrepreneurial spirit, Jim wondered whether profit would need to be split equally three ways. "We'll have to see," I evaded.

One day Jim announced that he had seen a new 16-inch Homecraft chainsaw that he was sure would be easier to handle than our old one. I was so pleased with his desire to learn lumberjacking that I went and bought the new toy. It started like a charm and had its own noseguard to prevent kickback. He soon mastered the craft of sawing away from the bind. We dug roots and rented a roto-tiller to plough up the patch. It was a busy fall between soccer, piano, homework and agriculture but we got the plot all ready before the November rains.

In early spring the project met with so much enthusiasm that I had to caution waiting until the soil was warm enough before planting corn and explained that some crops could be sown earlier than others. Even Marge came out the day we planted the corn. I was elated that I had won three converts.

But in the spring he did no tilling and no trimming back of the vines that grew rampant over the whole patch. And he sowed no corn. I gave up on nurturing his entrepreneurial spirit and felt he could always fall back on becoming a lawyer. One result of the cessation of the project was that our whole family enjoyed a tension-free summer.

Then one August day Jim brought in a first small bowl of blackberries. He announced, "Snowcrest is buying blackberries for 65 cents a pound. Can you bring some flats from town for me to fill?" Total profits for the season: $143.26.

HILDA J. BORN

Finding My Class

In 1949, to get my teaching credentials, I had to go to Normal School in Vancouver. Willa Witte from our Grade 13 class at Philip Sheffield was going too, so we decided to share an apartment. With a $125 bursary and my summer berry-picking money, I hoped to make it through the year.

I was eager to know the city. To do this I rode entire streetcar and bus routes on Sunday afternoons after settling in. Before long, I knew Vancouver better than some who'd grown up in the city.

Willa soon suggested that we'd save money if we helped in a home exchange for our room and board. We looked at the school advertising display and each found a place that wanted a live-in student. Mine was at a pediatrician's home. The families had probably checked our scholastic and character references and welcomed this unpaid house-keeping and childcare.

I was apprehensive about moving into a professional's home. The spare rural home in which I grew up was always neat and clean, but in 1949 we still did not have a telephone. I didn't know what to expect at this mansion in Shaughnessy. "Will the baby and toddler accept a stranger like me" I wondered. My little sister follows me around when-ever I'm home, and I hope these tiny ones will soon do the same."

The children adjusted to me more easily than I did to the opulent surroundings. One day, when I was washing a crystal bowl, the woman said, "Be careful with that, Hilda. It's from Europe and cost seven hun-dred dollars." I nearly dropped the bowl.

My eagerness to please and my fear of making mistakes added to my anxiety. There was reason for this. One evening, the doctor and his wife went to a concert and left me in charge. When I took the garbage out after supper, the door automatically locked behind me. I was terri-fied, but consoled to know that the babies were asleep upstairs. Fortunately, the neighbor I contacted had a key to let me in.

After two months I still felt tense. It was difficult to prepare for classes and also do everything that was expected of me in that home:

dusting; mopping the floor; vacuuming; washing and drying the dishes, then putting each dish in its precise place; and childcare—after school and whenever my employers went out. It was too much, and I decided to move elsewhere. "But Hilda, you're doing such a fine job," they said when I told them. "Won't you reconsider? We'd like to keep you here; we'll help you. We'd be willing to pay for your tuition." I thanked them cordially but declined, explaining, "I'm eager to finish my present course. With practice teaching next month, I'll need even more preparation time."

Before giving notice, I had checked the want ads for a place without babies. My next placement was with a shipping executive's family, the Tingleys. There were two children: Lael, six, and Philip, ten. My work after returning from classes included picking up the children's toys, ironing Mr. Tingley's shirts, washing supper dishes and caring for the children in their parents' absence.

The workload was similar in both places, but the atmosphere in the Tingley home was more relaxed, although, here too, I was not allowed to use their laundry facilities. Nor was I ever invited to share a meal with the family in either of these homes. I always ate alone in the kitchen. "Am I just a scullery maid?" I sometimes wondered as I ate my meal in silence.

I didn't blame them for wanting private family conversation during the dinner hour. However, it would have been nice to eat an occasional meal in the dining room. Still, my rank in the family birth order had partly conditioned me to accept such treatment, and I consoled myself with thoughts such as, "at home I can never be first either, I'm always the third Klassen daughter."

It wasn't that the Tingleys didn't trust me. When they went on a ten-day business trip to San Diego, the children and two dogs were left in my care. On their return, I received a thank-you gift of a twelve-inch square of brown and turquoise polyester. At first I didn't know what to do with it. But then I realized: by stretching it into a neckerchief, I could embellish my meager wardrobe.

Occasionally I had a weekend off. To go home on Friday, I rode the BC Hydro tram to Clayburn. On Sunday evening I returned to Vancouver by Greyhound and city bus. I walked the last six blocks carrying my suitcase; inside was my clean laundry. Usually this was a late bus, long after dark. But nobody ever bothered me.

During my spare time I went to the Girls' Home on 43rd Street. It was a safe place for single young women, mostly Mennonite, to relax and meet friends. Many came from farming families in the Fraser Valley and helped out by taking housekeeping jobs in the city; a few of us were students.

When I didn't go home for the weekend, I also attended the church nearby. With all the moves and changes in my last three years, I felt a need for spiritual nourishment. Because I didn't have free time to go to choir practice, I was glad when the Easter program committee asked me to recite a Resurrection poem. I wanted to participate, but knew I'd be facing a sea of strangers. "Lord, keep me calm so I don't stumble over any words!" I prayed. The poem was seven stanzas long. Both the matrons of the Girls' Home and the minister were pleased, so my prayer was answered.

With spring came teacher-hiring time. I was included in the group of 35 teachers who were offered jobs in Vancouver. Without hesitation, I declined. I had always visualized myself as a rural pioneer and was eager to see and experience life in the hinterlands.

A telegram soon arrived with an offer to teach in Rock Creek. I wanted to jump at the chance to go up-country. My father promptly vetoed that. "Not until you are 21 years old," he insisted. It was the legal age then, and naturally I obeyed him. I balled up that telegram but kept it. Soon after, I applied for a position closer to home. At that time you could not begin teaching in the area where you had last attended school, so Mission and Abbotsford were out for me. This rule applied despite the fact that I'd only moved here recently and attended Philip Sheffield for only one year.

I was appointed to Otter School in Langley district. When the yellow buses rolled up in September, I welcomed 42 expectant faces into my classroom.

RICK MAWSON

With a Cultural Twist

Nirmal lives upstairs. Before I fall asleep each night, I listen to his gentle and sometimes robust snores.

I think Nirmal sleeps on the floor, perhaps on a pallet or a blanket, as the sounds seem so close to the ground, and the ceiling creaks and protests under his shifting, yet not very substantial weight. The purr of his snore often progresses to a strangled roar by 11 p.m., then descends in gradual stages to an insubstantial hum by midnight.

Nirmal and several other members of his family live upstairs: his wife, his young son; his daughter-in-law and his new baby grandson, who is the pride and joy of Nirmal's life. I know this from the soft cooing sounds he makes to calm the infant each time a bout of prolonged shrieking threatens to break out; and from the times I have seen them together in the back garden, the old man holding the child aloft, way, way above his head, showing him the world he has only recently dropped into.

Another time I sit and watch from my window as the boy is introduced by his grandfather to the drowsy, cud-munching cows in the spring field at the end of our street.

Nirmal lives upstairs. And quite often, by chance, we meet each other as I return from my evening jog, or he from his early morning walk. We are separated by language and cultural barriers thousands of years and miles apart, but despite this, we strive manfully to communicate across such vast distances. Perhaps it would be more accurate to say that Nirmal strives. He is the one swimming in an unfamiliar and treacherous sea of English.

"Ah, hello, Mr. Rick!" offers Nirmal bravely, as I limp back into the driveway, soaked and bedraggled after five-mile trot down the Hope River Road during the height of the B.C. monsoon season. "Hello, Mr. Rick. Today ... today, it is very much ... weather!"

"Yes, yes," I agree, "today it is certainly very much weather!" I know he is intent on improving his English. I see him walking in the garden on sunny days, his English books in his hands, repeating words and phrases that must seem difficult and perplexing to him. But he is persistent and he won't give up easily.

"Mr. Rick," he continues, the desire to communicate almost palpable between us, "you are running every day like this?"

"No, no," I reply, "just three or four times a week, whenever I have the time or inclination." I try to explain that if I'm not able to run for three or four days in a row, I miss it and feel irritable and out of sorts. This confuses him and his brow wrinkles in concern.

"You do not feel good, Mr. Rick? But why do you, then ... do it?"

In fractured English accompanied by sign language, I struggle to get across to him that I'm really quite okay, that my body likes the feeling it gets when I'm running and that if I stop, it misses it. "Running," I say, "is good for me." Nirmal's eyes light up with comprehension.

"Oh, yes, yes. It is good, very good, Mr. Rick. It is ... most good!"

There is an awkward pause. For the moment, we have exhausted our subject and our communication skills. The rain is dripping from my drenched track suit, and the delicious, warm smell of an East Indian curry beckons to him from the upstairs apartment where his grandson has just begun his evening serenade.

We stand for a few moments, two reluctant solitudes yearning to discuss in a leisurely way the burning issues of the day: the free trade deal, was it a good move? Will Canada survive as a nation beyond the turn of the century? Is Brian Mulroney an extra-terrestrial with a sick sense of humor? But all we manage is, "Goodnight, Mr. Rick" and "Goodnight, Nirmal," as we return to our separate worlds within one building.

I go inside, somewhat dejected, and contemplate a crash course in Punjabi as I take a hot shower to erase the chill brought on by our epic conversation in the rain.

Nirmal lives upstairs with his son, Rajinder, a sawmill worker who has recently been laid off, and his handsome, dark-eyed daughter-in-law. Both were born in India but have been brought up in Canada and speak good English. Rajinder and I often have short, probing bouts of conversation in passing.

Today, when I go upstairs to pay the rent, Rajinder proudly shows me his rec-room which he has just finished drywalling, and the new fireplace in his living room. His wife smiles demurely and offers me a dish of spicy Indian tidbits to take back with me to my apartment, while her chubby infant son stares me with wide, white-brown, button eyes that flash fear and fascination for the strange, pink, whiskered face that has emerged from the bowels of the house.

The house is often filled with noise, music, and raised voices speaking at speed, as well as with tantalizing smells when other members of Nirmal's family pay weekend or holiday visits. I'm surprised that this mayhem fails to annoy me. Previous apartments with their noisy occupants often drove me to distraction and bouts of fruitless wall-hammering, but here I find this familial cacophony curiously welcome.

A female friend from Vancouver pays me a visit for the weekend. Nirmal corners her in the garden, eager to test his English and satisfy his curiosity. "You are the lady friend of Mr. Rick?" he enquires diplomatically, painfully unsure of the intricacies of western male-female relationships. "You are working here in Chilliwack?" he continues, still eager for information. "A teacher? Oh dear. Too much money, too much money," and he shakes his head, smiling, overcome by largesse of the B.C. taxpayer.

"Mr. Rick," confides Nirmal to my friend, "is a very fine man. Mr. Rick is a … a gentleman!" And then he quickly invites her to learn the secret art of chapatti making from his daughter-in-law.

I want to tell him that I think he is a gentleman, too, but I find it difficult. I know that he found it much easier to relay his impressions of me through a third party. We live cheek by jowl, and yet know so little of each other.

I want to sit down with Nirmal over a dish of Madras curry and talk about life and death, and marriage and God, and pain and pride, and prejudice and friendship—and gentlemen. I want to know the story of his life in India, how and why he came to Canada and what he thinks of it here. But instead we exchange occasional pleasantries, barely scratching the surface of a mutual understanding.

This evening, I watch him from my ground floor window as he sits guru-like in the back garden, his grandson on his knee, paying quiet homage to the sun as it sets. Ten minutes earlier on the six o'clock news, I have seen a young East Indian man jailed for life for the murder of his sister and her husband who had eloped and married without familial consent.

The young man's father could be Nirmal's twin brother; the same proud, patriarchial carriage, the same intelligent, dark eyes that in this case are dulled with suffering and bewilderment, unlike the cheerful,

148

mischievous gaze I'm used to seeing Nirmal turn on the world. Such pain and passion, I think, such wisdom and mirth inhabiting the same features.

For a brief moment, judgment blinds me, and I find myself wondering if I have idealized Nirmal, turning him into something or someone he is not, just to suit my own whimsical, romantic view of his race. The answer arrives swiftly, with the reproving sting of a well-needed slap to the intellect: it really doesn't matter. What does matter is, Nirmal lives upstairs, and I would like very much to be his friend.

WENDY E. BURTON

Swimming Winter's Lake

When I swim the winter lake, I go for heart's sake. Stepping naked from the sweat lodge, I am greeted by the water, and steam rises like benediction into the chill air. I swim forward into a lake as dark as the mysteries, and all that will warm me is the heat of my blood pounding like the drums I hear from the beach. Most turn back, but I swim the shoreline of the lake, a giant's circle. My arm rising and falling, my thighs beating against the walls of frigid water, soon the only sound is the boom of my own heart.

My companion becomes my curved right arm as I inhale the icy air and see the ancient trees crowding this mountain lake. Hypothermia in 20 minutes, the scientist tells me. Yet I swim, my eyes soon sightless to anything but the harbour of my right arm, the only sound the inhaled chill air. I exhale into water, and the bubbles stretch away to deep and bitter dark where no light falls and no warmth comes. I swim, stroke after stroke, a rhythm so old it comes to me with messages of fire and community, and I swim as my sisters swam, to rid myself of winter spirits and to greet the spring. I swim, my body a challenge to this dark and brooding cold, this chill of winter death, to bring spring to the waiting land and to me.

As the farthest point, a half-mile out, 30 minutes out, beyond sight and hearing, I am beyond heart's endurance and the cold waits for me to falter, to be afraid. "You can't do this," the shadows beneath me sigh. As I dream men and women singing in the longhouse, the canoe pullers begin to chant me home.

I dream; I drift. My heart's steady boom becomes the rocking of my in-held breath, and panic starts to chatter because I am a small creature defying winter's lake and it's true I can't do this and then that blazing defiance, that fire, re-kindles at the base of my ribs. I release my breath, blow life into the lake, lift arm and head and inhale, and steadily, fiercely return to the beach where the drum calls and measures and answers the booming chant of my heart that is – at last – all that is to be heard in this solitary place.

LOIS J. PETERSON

Stopping at High River

I'd last run away from home when I was seven, taking my shorn Barbie, an unopened package of colored plastic clothes pins, and a handful of bills from my father's dresser. An hour later when my mother brought me home, she explained that I'd taken the hoard of Italian money saved from their honeymoon eleven years before and I'd not have been able to spend it.

This time, I took nothing. After a trip to Safeway to pick up some things for supper, I glanced one way, then pulled out into the traffic going in the opposite direction. I threw the ground chicken and box of pasta in the garbage can in the 7-11 parking lot when I stopped for coffee two hours later outside Chilliwack. By the time I got to Boston Bar all I could think of was a huge plate of breakfast, slick with griddle fat, a bottomless cup of coffee, both of which Lorraine gave me without registering any surprise or curiosity about why I was there.

Even though we'd not seen each other in eleven years I'd have recognized her thick eyebrows anywhere. When I fetched up at the High River Restaurant, thirsty after the long day's drive, led along only by the road and the need to turn my back on something I had tired of, without knowing what I had to look forward to, she peered at me, then stepped back and laughed. "Well, look at you. When I said you should drop by, I never figured you'd take me up on it. Looking for work?"

She was kidding, but I answered, 'Sure. I can serve, even if I can't cook."

In the days since then I've poured coffee and folded paper napkins, swabbed the scuffed floor and stacked menus, falling into a dull sleep in the storeroom at the back of the building after Lorraine steers her Mustang out onto the highway for the two-mile drive home.

She hasn't asked me why I left, why I chose to show up on her doorstep, why I haven't moved on yet, and where I'd go if I did. And I see no point in trying to explain to someone who longs for the kind of life I'd been living, that I couldn't stay for another ten years with a man who asks me what shirt to wear when we go out for Sunday brunch, or where we keep the Band-Aids.

I can't admit that since we'd last seen each other I've become the kind of wife I'd always despised, throwing oblique questions about what time my husband will be home - although I don't really care where he was going—making his lunch, every day the same bologna and mustard, never asking what else he might prefer. Never being told.

While I've waited here, I've often walked through the restaurant parking lot, down the slope through the sparse apple trees, to the scrawny riverside park below. Heaps of rusty rocks hunker along the opposite banks, twisted sagebrush nestles between the gullies the rain has driven through the canyon soil.

I've basked in the heat thrown from the canyon face, inhaling dry air, as I've tried to imagine a life here, tending apples and tomatoes to sell to highway travellers driving East or West. Waiting tables, going to bed each night in the small room down the long hall where the thrum of fridges packed with bagged coleslaw and jugs of ketchup drown out my dreams.

Groups of whitewater rafters often barge past, swigging beer, leaning back into the wind, their voices ramming the cliff walls as they call back and forth to each other. I took that same trip years ago, through the dark pools of Hell's Gate. Sitting against the pontoons of swollen rubber, I studied the Fraser's steep sides from below, and went home with a sunburn, but with no greater sense of the where I'd been than when I left.

The narrow park, a few hundred yards of gravel and dust, follows the line of the river. Planted into the rocks by roots of cement are picnic benches, garbage cans, and barbecue pits, almost all unused so early in the season. Big rigs and recreational vehicles thunder along the highway above, throwing up clouds of dust, flocks of fast food wrappers. A slow but steady stream of crumpled travelers stop at the café for chef salads and chips and milk shakes, but Lorraine seems to spend more time at the window than the griddle, breathing in the relative peace before summer brings overloaded cars of parents hauling freckled kids, nestled in amongst sleeping bags, coolers and lawn chairs.

Each morning, I've woken in the bare room, and felt the ground shudder from the passing traffic. Like the river below the restaurant, it only slows from time to time, but never rests.

It's taken my husband only five days to find me.
I find him reading a menu at a window table when I come in from cleaning the washroom. I detour past the counter, pick up a half-full carafe,

152

and walk over to his table. "Coffee?"

He pushes a cup towards me. "That all you have to say?" His eyes are in deep shadow, a patch of stubble, like smoke, smudges his cheek. I pour his coffee, set the jug on the table beside his ashtray. Just as I'm about to ask if he wants something to eat, Lorraine swoops past in a rustle of peach nylon. She grabs the coffee. "I'll take that. We do have a few customers, you know."

Geoff's gaze follows her as she weaves between empty tables. "You left this number on the kitchen table."

"But…"

"A buddy at Telus looked up the address."

Geoff's buddies can get you a seat on a full flight, or cheap camping gear long after the sale's over. Over the years, I've become just one more good deal. There's nothing left between us of the heat of yearning, of a gaze that's always restless until it finds home in the eyes of someone it loves.

My husband's told me over and over that he doesn't mind about the children, gone before they were even named. But we've dandled too many silences between us like babies with no solid surface on which to place them.

"I'd have figured you'd have gone to the Island," Geoff says.

"I like it here." Only as I speak the words, do I realize they are true. There's no room for artifice in Lorraine's world. Customers come and go, eat and pay up, tip or don't bother. Every few nights her boyfriend calls from whatever pit stop he's parked his rig in, and she complains about receipts, recounts how the griddle caught on fire, asks whether he thinks she should let Jo Moss leave his van out front, just until he gets the manifold fixed. Then I hear the smoky rattle of her laugh as she lowers her voice, and when she turns from hanging up the phone, she'll be blushing.

The restaurant is clean but shabby, the cabinet under the glass counter empty except for a sprawl of faded road maps and a half-empty box of breath mints. But the food's good enough to bring customers back on their return journey, and since my first day, I find I'm happy spending time between orders watching the dark stream of coffee trail from the stainless cone into the glass pitcher below.

"You hungry?" I ask my husband.

Geoff scrubs the palm of one hand across his face, and through his fingers I hear him say, "Where're you staying, then?"

He follows me along the narrow hallway, past the bulletin board of faded signs advertising backhoe services, a Friday night whist game. We lay down on top of the sleeping bag, and hold each other for a long time without speaking. He's still wearing his shoes, and my slick uniform fills the narrow space between us like water we cannot cross.

"What would it take?" he mutters into my shoulder.

I know he's asking me to come home, but doesn't know how.

"Too much." I feel his deep shuddering sigh against me. Then we both sleep.

Later, after Lorraine has made Geoff an omelet which I serve him garnished with a sprig of parsley, we walk down to the park and sit on the dusty picnic table.

I watch the breeze seep through the cottonwood leaves overhead. "We were going to travel. Why didn't we?"

Geoff's reply is tossed away by a gust of wind and he doesn't bother to retrieve it. I gaze up towards the highway, counting passing vehicles until he speaks again.

He asks me what he should do about my sewing machine, and the new end tables that are to be delivered on Thursday. He says nothing about my job, and I don't ask what he'll tell his mother whose fierceness I'd always loved, even though I've always been slightly afraid of her. Glenda would not approve of wives who leave their husbands and hole up in highway restaurants: I know she'll use her disappointment as the knife to slice me out of her life.

I think about the petunias I planted under the kitchen window, and the screens Geoff needs to hose down before he puts them back on the windows. His new pants are still in the sewing basket waiting to be shortened.

But I say nothing. I've already given up the right to mention these things, although it's all we've ever had to talk about.

Soon after we met in Port Coquitlam, when we were too young and nervous to discuss what mattered, even if we'd been able to identify it, we went to a dance in the Agricultural Hall. Geoff held me against him, the planes of our bodies resting against each other, devoid of promise but still comforting and somehow familiar. I remember how his hand slid up the small of my back, slick against the fabric of my dress, in the same way his hand, older now, rougher and scarred, moved up my body as we lay together for the last time on the cot in the room behind the

154

kitchen. Long ago on the creaking dance floor, the music shaking the walls, we'd found nothing to say to each other.

"Why did we never go dancing?" I ask. "Not since that first time. Remember that time at the Aggie Hall?"

"Didn't know you wanted to," he says.

Above us, an eagle wheels in the thermals, then turns to follow the river glittering between steep shady banks.

Although I love it here in the restaurant hanging above the valley, I can't stay. The place is hung with a film of grease, and in a couple of months there'll be no peace even down by the river. The heat will glaze the valley and the travellers' faces with a dense silence that will be too familiar to be comfortable.

Gravel crunches under our feet as we walk back up the slope. We stop beside the red Acura Geoff bought home one Saturday without consulting me. I lean against the passenger door for a moment, wondering what it would take to lean down and grasp the handle, open the door, and ease myself in.

A truck pulls up, throwing out gravel and dust. Geoff coughs and wipes his hand down his cheek. "Where will you be, then? Just in case."

I turn one way, then the other, trying to imagine the place where the ribbon of road runs out. But I have nothing on which to base an image of the landscape in either direction. "Here, for now. I guess. A day or so, maybe."

Lorraine is knocking on the window; she's been on her feet since five, and will be wanting a break before the supper traffic rolls in. I shrug at her, then turn back to my husband who for just one moment smiles in the guileless way he first looked at me from the scrum of a game his team was about to lose. But then replacing the brief smile I see something that might be the glitter of tears, or just the sun's reflection in his eyes.

I pat the front of his shirt, not letting my hand rest long enough to register the heat from below the fabric. I'd like to tell him I'm sorry. But it's too late to start lying. Instead, I lean forward and place a dry kiss on his cheek.

As I watch his car turn out of the parking lot, slowing for a moment before Geoff eases into the traffic, I think of the women who've told me they'd leave it all, start again, if they could. If they knew how.

Understanding their fear, I stand in the only place that matters, while the dust of the highway billows out in both directions.

About the Contributors

Nola Accili is a French instructor at the University College of the Fraser Valley. Previously, she has taught at Simon Fraser University, and has been published in *The Lyric.*

A homegrown girl and mother from 100 Mile House, **Kristine Archie** is inspired by mountains, handshakes, smiles and UCFV English profs. She currently studies at the University of Victoria.

Michael Aird lives in White Rock, and teaches on the Lower Mainland. His work has most recently appeared in *The Fiddlehead.*

Allan Bailey was raised in Langley. He studied Japanese and earned his PhD in Education from UBC. Currently, he currently divides his time between Kyoto's Ritsumeikan University where he teaches English, and White Rock.

Ranbir Banwait is working on her BA in English with a minor in Applied Ethical and Political Philosophy at UCFV. Her work is dedicated to capturing the beauty of life in art and writing.

 Dave Bennett is an Aldergrove writer. A former journalist, his previous fiction has appeared in *Futures Mysterious Anthology Magazine,* for which he is also an editorial reader.

Hilda J. Born lives in Abbotsford. She tells more travel and life stories in *Maria's Century, You Are Wherever You Go,* and *Walking With Hope.*

J. M. Bridgeman has an M.A. in Literature from the University of Manitoba. She moved to the Fraser Valley in 1989. Her book *Here In Hope: A Natural History* is published by Oolichan.

Leslie J. Bryant was born in Rosedale in 1924. He raised pure-bred Hereford cattle for more than 50 years, and served as a 4-H Club leader. He writes on Rosedale's community history.

A poverty and justice issues activist, **Wendy E. Burton** was conceived during the Fraser Valley's great flood of 1948. She returned there in 1979 to teach workplace writing and adult education.

John Carroll lives at Yarrow. A writer, director, actor and educator, his collection of poems, *Rumour Of a Shark* (1999), is published by Barbarian Press.

Ron Dart teaches political science, philosophy & religious studies at UCFV. He has published four books of poetry, two on the Canadian High Tory political tradition, and one on poet Robin Mathews.

Crispin Elsted is a poet, essayist, translator, compositor, and publisher, and has also worked as an actor, a musician, and a bearward. His book *Climate & the Affections: Poems 1970-1995* (Sono Nis, 1996) was short-listed for the Governor General's Award.

Alvin G. Ens writes poetry, short fiction and the occasional short non-fiction. An English teacher, he has published *Musings on the Sermon*, a book of meditative religious verse.

Kuldip Gill was born in Punjab, and attended school in the Fraser Valley. She worked in forestry and mining for 20 years, and taught anthropology at UBC and SFU. Her latest book, *Valley Sutra*, is published by Beach Holme. Other works include: *Dharma Rasa*; *Cornelian, Turquoise and Gold*; and *Ghazals: Rai and Sohni*.

Vicki Grieve is a recent graduate of SFU's Writer's Studio Program at Harbour Centre. She lives in Chilliwack, not far from where she grew up, and teaches at UCFV.

A renovator-painter, **Shelley Haggard** was born in Fort St. John and lived on Vancouver Island for twelve years before settling in the Fraser Valley. She enjoys tole-painting and photography.

Born in 1928, **Hilda Harder** was raised in the valley's Ridgedale area. While growing up, she spent much time in the Crippled Children's Hospital. She now lives in Abbotsford.

After decades living away, **Douglas Isaac** recently resettled on a farm at Mount Lehman. His works include *Past, Present: Tense...*, a satiric, epic narrative of his search through history for his Mennonite heritage, and a novel, *Altered Biography: The Womb Years* (Arsenal/Pulp).

Trudi Jarvis' family ran the Hunter Creek BA truck stop from 1947-1971. She grew up watching tugboats work the local booming grounds and still lives at Laidlaw overlooking the Fraser River.

A former teacher, **May La Chance** lives in Chilliwack where her family arrived about 1874 and logged in the valley through the 1920s. Her grandfather, Dr. George Fife, pioneered the Langley- Surrey area in 1900.

Helen Grace Lescheid is mother of five grown children, a retired nurse and a writer. Her work has appeared in *Reader's Digest, The Province* and *Guideposts.* She lives in Abbotsford.

A sports enthusiast, **Cameron Little** graduated from UCFV. He is currently enrolled in the B.C. Teachers certification program at University of Victoria.

Robert Martens grew up in the Mennonite village of Yarrow, BC, moved on to the turbulent politics of Simon Fraser University in the seventies, and eventually settled quietly in Abbotsford.

A member of UCFV's Theatre department, **Rick Mawson** was born in England and moved to Canada in 1974. His play, *Caliban: House-Sitter* was a hit of the 2000 Vancouver Fringe Festival.

Rose Morrison teaches Agricultural Science at UCFV: "across continents / through earth scents, loves and children / poems come at last."

Elsie K. Neufeld is a recipient of the Abbotsford Arts Council Award for Outstanding Literary Achievement. An article about her appeared in *The Beaver*, Canada's history magazine, in 2004.

Peggy Sue Neufeld was raised in northern B.C. where her father trapped and sold furs to the Hudson Bay Company. Of Cree ancestry, she has published in *The Whitehorse Star* and in Fraser Valley community newspapers. She lives in Hope.

Walter Neufeld lives in B.C. but works in Calgary during the week. He is an active member of Boardwalk Writers and The Society of Poets, Bards and Storytellers in Calgary, and reads regularly at local venues.

Lois J. Peterson's stories, essays, and articles are widely published in Canada, the US and UK. She operates LPwordsolutions, a writing and editing company, and teaches for the Surrey Creative Writing Diploma Program

Poet and novelist **Marion Quednau** lives in Mission. Her chapbook, *Kissing: Selected Chronicles* won the League of Canadian Poets Chapbook Award in 1999. Her poems appear in *The Common Sky: Canadian Writers against the War*, and *Listening with the Ear of the Heart*.

Al Rempel grew up in the Fraser Valley and now lives in an intentional community in Prince George. Several of his poems were published in the August, 2004 issue of *Grain*.

Andreas Schroeder is the author of over 20 books of fiction, creative non-fiction, poetry and history. He holds the Maclean-Hunter Chair in Creative Non-Fiction in UBC's Creative Writing Department

Julia van Gorder lives in the sky by Stanley Park.

Born and raised in the Fraser Valley, **Martin VanWoudenberg** spends his time designing web pages, writing poety and fiction, and being a husband and father.

Janet Vickers is a student in the BA in Adult Education program at UCFV. Her poems have appeared in *sub-Terrain, The Common Sky: Canadian Writers Against the War*, and *Grain*.

Donald White is now 72 years old and living in Chilliwack. He still works full time as a rural mail carrier in the Cultus Lake, Columbia Valley area.